Mountain Peaks
of Christ

By
Tom Malone, D.D., Th.D.

Sword of the Lord Publishers
Murfreesboro, Tennessee

ISBN 0-87398-562-1

Printed and bound in the United States of America

Contents

DR. TOM MALONE

INTRODUCTION

When Tom Malone left the home of his grandparents to attend Bob Jones College in Cleveland, Tennessee (now Bob Jones University in Greenville, South Carolina), he was determined to learn to preach. He carried with him a small hope-it-don't-rain cardboard suitcase. It contained a few clothes and—of all things—a pillow!

That pillow just may have been symbolic.

When young Jacob of olden times left home he met God at Bethel. It was there he dreamed of the heavenly ladder with angels ascending and descending. It was there he received assurance from the Lord God that he would be blessed and would be a blessing to many. All of this Jacob dreamed as he lay with his head pillowed upon a stone he had found in that place.

When young Tom of modern times left home he fully expected that he, too, would be blessed of God and would, in turn, be a blessing to others. He not only expected to dream dreams—he even took along his own pillow!

Through these good years it has been characteristic of the man to expect the blessing and power of God upon his ministry. He always has that pillow handy that he may be ready for God to give him other dreams and visions.

It is doubtful, though, if young Malone ever dreamed of becoming the man he is today. He is now Doctor Tom Malone, is renowned in fundamental circles for his wise leadership and great preaching, is pastor of the large Emmanuel Baptist Church of Pontiac, Michigan, is founder and president of Midwestern Baptist College, and is eagerly sought as speaker in large Bible conferences from coast to coast.

Dr. John R. Rice has often said that Dr. Tom Malone may be the greatest gospel preacher in all the world today!

Of course, like other men mightily used of God, he has paid a dear price for this ministry. Only he and his lovely wife know what it has cost in prayer, preparation, downright hard work, and tears. But, on the other hand, only he and

Mrs. Malone know how rich have been the rewards of faithful soul winning and Bible teaching.

In this book are sermons that Dr. Malone has preached from his pulpit in Pontiac. You will be blessed by them because they are based on scriptural truth with quotations again and again from the Bible. You will enjoy them because of the many heart-warming stories that are told to illustrate these great Bible truths. These sermons cover the great events in the life of Christ: His virgin birth, His baptism, His transfiguration, His triumphal entry into Jerusalem, His sacrificial death, His resurrection, His ascension and His second coming.

This is preaching that is characteristic of Tom Malone's ministry. And this is the kind of preaching that made America great. This is the kind of preaching that brings revival.

The reading of this book will warm your heart, instruct your mind, strengthen your faith and change your life.

We trust that these sermons will cause many another youngster to pack a pillow in his suitcase—and start out to do great things for God!

Dr. Bill Rice.

THE INSPIRATION OF THE BIBLE

"The writing was the writing of God."—Exod. 32:16.
"These are the true sayings of God."—Rev. 19:9.

I. Why Preach on the Inspiration of the Bible
1. Because of Those Who Deny It
2. Because of Those Who Dissect It
3. Because of Those Who Disregard It
4. Because of Those Who Would Desecrate It
5. Because of Those Who Delight in It

II. Why I Believe the Bible Infallibly Inspired
1. I Believe in the Inspiration of the Bible According to the Testimony of Jesus Christ
2. I Believe in the Inspiration of the Bible Because of Its Testimony of Fulfilled Prophecy
3. I Believe in the Inspiration of the Bible Because of Its Indestructibility
4. I Believe in the Inspiration of the Bible Because of Its Unparalleled Unity
5. I Believe in the Inspiration of the Bible Because of the Testimony of Its Transforming Power
6. I Believe in the Inspiration of the Bible Because of Its Inexhaustibility
7. I Believe in the Inspiration of the Bible Because of an Inward Witness

An Ancient Scroll of the Law
A copy of the Pentateuch, inscribed on lambskin and
prepared in the form of a scroll

1

The Inspiration of the Bible

"The writing was the writing of God."—Exod. 32:16.
"These are the true sayings of God."—Rev. 19:9.

These two statements out of the Bible are my text today:
"The writing was the writing of God" and, "These are the
true sayings of God." Now you may ask me, "Preacher,
why are you preaching on the inspiration of the Bible?"
There are at least five reasons why I believe it is necessary to preach on the inspiration of the Bible or why and
how I know that this is the Book of God and why we believe
that it is inspired.

I. WHY PREACH ON THE INSPIRATION OF THE BIBLE

1. Because of Those Who Deny It

I doubt if there has ever been an age in the history of
mankind when there were more people who literally out-
and-out deny the truth of God's Word. Of course, it is no
new thing. It started in the third chapter of Genesis when
Satan came in the garden where Adam and Eve were and
raised this question, "Yea, hath God said?" (Gen. 3:1).
People have been raising that question these hundreds and
thousands of years, "Yea, hath God said?" Is this the Book
of God or not? Does this Bible contain the Word of God or
is it the Word of God? That is the battle of the ages. So I
preach on this this morning because of those who deny it.

2. Because of Those Who Dissect It

I preach on it this morning in the second place because of
those who want to dissect it. People say, "Well, now
Preacher, I am going to admit to you that there is some of

the Bible that I believe is the Word of God, but there is some of it I do not believe is the accurate Word of God." For instance, some people take Genesis and say, "You cannot interpret the book of Genesis literally." They do not want to accept the Genesis account of the origin of man as the direct creation of God. Evolutionists are against the book of Genesis. There are those who want to take the book of Jonah where a miracle took place—a man was swallowed by a great fish and lived three days and came out preaching —out of the Bible. They say about the book of Daniel, "There is more than one language in the book of Daniel and we do not believe the book of Daniel is true." They want to say there were two authors of the book of Isaiah. They are like that old wicked king Jehoiakim back in the Old Testament, in Jeremiah, chapter 36. He had someone read him the Bible. He would read a page and Jehoiakim would take and cut that part out with a penknife. He would say, "Cut that part," and he would throw it in the fire and burn it up. They would read some more and he would take his penknife and cut that out and throw it in the fire. So there are those who dissect it.

3. Because of Those Who Disregard It

I preach this morning on the inspiration of the Bible because there are those who disregard it. Remember, my friends, that Jesus said, "Ye shall know the truth, and the truth shall make you free" (John 8:32). So I preach on the inspiration of the Bible this morning because so many people absolutely disregard the blessed Word of God.

4. Because of Those Who Would Desecrate It

I preach on the Bible this morning because of those who would desecrate it. There are those who would take from it. There are those who would add to it. If you would study the false religions of our day, you would be astonished how many either seek to take away or add to the blessed Book of God.

For instance, the Seventh-Day Adventists will refer you to the writings of Mrs. White and say that those writings are just as inspired as this Bible. The Christian Scientists will refer you to the writings of Mary Baker Patterson Glover Eddy, if I have remembered the names of all her husbands, and tell you that her book on *Science and Health, the Key to the Scriptures*, is just as inspired as the Bible. Mormons today will tell you that the writings on the so-called Copper Plates discovered in the origin of their religion is just as inspired as the Bible. Revelation 22:18 and 19 says:

"For I testify unto every man that heareth the words of the prophecy of this book, If any man shall add unto these things, God shall add unto him the plagues that are written in this book: And if any man shall take away from the words of the book of this prophecy, God shall take away his part out of the book of life, and out of the holy city, and from the things which are written in this book."

I preach today on the inspiration of the Bible because of those who would desecrate it.

5. Because of Those Who Delight in It

But, I am preaching mainly this morning on the inspiration of the Bible because of those who delight in it. I thank God that there are yet hundreds and thousands of old-fashioned, born-again, blood-washed people of God all over this world who revere this blessed Book and look upon it as the Book that God wrote. "The writing was...of God."

Many times in the Bible there are those who expressed great love for the blessed Word of God. For instance, the psalmist David said, "O how love I thy law! it is my meditation all the day" (Ps. 119:97). David said, "How sweet are thy words unto my taste! yea, sweeter than honey to my mouth!" (Ps. 119:103). You see, Bible-believing Christians, really born-again people, believe the Bible and love the Bible and know the Bible is inspired of God and is God's holy Word.

I would say to you this morning, first of all, there is no shadow of doubt, this Bible claims to be the Book of God. For instance, in Luke 1:70 we read, "As he spake by the mouth of his holy prophets, which have been since the world began." God says this Book is what "God spake by the mouth of his holy prophets." I read in II Timothy 3:16, "All Scripture is given by inspiration of God...." The word "inspiration" comes from two Latin words, *in* and *spiro—inspiro.* It means "to breathe into," and II Timothy 3:16 says, "All scripture"—that includes the book of Jonah; "All scripture" —that includes the book of Genesis; "All scripture"—that includes all the parts you cannot understand; "All scripture" —that includes the parts that seem to be contradictory; "All scripture is given by inspiration of God...." I read again in II Peter 1:21, "For the prophecy came not in old time by the will of man: but holy men of God spake as they were moved by the Holy Ghost."

This Bible claims that it is the voice of God and that the Holy Spirit is doing the speaking. I am not going to take the time to define the difference between inspiration and illumination and interpretation or revelation. I merely want to show you why I believe and why every Christian ought to believe with all of his heart and all of his life that this Bible is the inspired Book of God.

Someone has defined inspiration, and it is about the best human definition of inspiration I have ever heard:

> Inspiration denotes that secret action of the Spirit on the faculties of a living messenger by which he is enabled to receive, utter or record the divine message. Scripture is the result of that sacred influence, embodied and recorded in written form.

So you see this Bible claims God spoke through the minds

and hearts of men to give us a complete revelation of Himself.

I asked Mrs. Malone, before we were married, to copy a poem in the first new Bible I had after I was saved (except for a little dime store Bible I took to college with me which I used for preaching and holding revivals). She wrote this little poem in it and it has been dear to my heart all these years.

> This precious Book, I'd rather own
>   Than all the golden gems
> That ever in monarch's coffers shone,
>   Than all their diadems.
> Nay, were the sea a chrysolite,
>   The earth a golden ball,
> And diamonds all the stars of night,
>   This Book were worth them all.

For these thirty-three years I have preached with the deep conviction that wherever I read, whatever book, whatever chapter, whatever line, whatever word, whatever syllable, I am preaching the inspired Word of Almighty God written by the Holy Ghost Himself. Job 23:12 says, "...I have esteemed the words of his mouth more than my necessary food." Job said, "God's Word means more to me than food for my body. This is better than breakfast; better than lunch; it is better than supper." Job said, "...I have esteemed the words of his mouth more than my necessary food." Someone has said:

> Christ is the grand object of the Bible; our good its design and the glory of God its end. A mine of wealth, a paradise of glory and a river of pleasure. It is given you in life, it will be opened in judgment and remembered forever. It involves the highest responsibility, will reward the greatest labor and condemn all who trifle with its sacred contents.

I want you to be reminded today, not only does God honor and bless those who believe this Bible and hold it sacred, but God has promised to judge those people who condemn and desecrate and doubt the Word of God as the inspired Bible.

They are doing it today in colleges all over America. I am preaching to families this morning whose young people will go away to some state institution and before long some Ph.D., educated far beyond his intelligence, will be telling them that it is archaic and old-fashioned to believe the Bible. Then with words smoother than butter, and with his brilliance, but lack of faith and judgment, he will destroy the faith the young people have in the blessed Book of God.

Now, why do I believe in the verbal inspiration of the Bible? I mean by that, the words, the plenary verbal inspiration of the Bible, that is, the full verbal inspiration of the Bible as it was in its original manuscripts? Why do I believe this morning in the inspiration, the total, complete, verbal inspiration of the blessed Word of God? I have seven reasons.

II. WHY I BELIEVE THE BIBLE INFALLIBLY INSPIRED

1. I Believe in the Inspiration of the Bible According to the Testimony of Jesus Christ

First of all, I believe in the inspiration of the Bible according to the testimony of Jesus Christ. In John 5:39 Jesus said, "Search the scriptures; for in them ye think ye have eternal life...." Jesus spoke of the Scriptures when He said, "Search the scriptures; for in them ye think ye have eternal life...." I would like to show you this morning—or let the Lord show you—how the Lord Jesus Christ took His hand and put His stamp of approval on every single book, every single one of the sixty-six books in this blessed Word of God. I would like for you to see this morning out of the Bible where Jesus from Genesis to Revelation said, "I approve of this Book as the inspired Word of God."

First of all, I read where Jesus did it in Luke 24:27, "And beginning at Moses and all the prophets, he expounded unto them in all the scriptures the things concerning himself." So Jesus put His seal of approval on all of the Old Testament. (I will get to the New Testament in a moment.) Take, for instance, the book of Jonah. People say, "Why, only a fool would believe that old-fashioned book that says that a fish swallowed a man and he lived inside that fish three days and when he got out, he went to Nineveh and preached." I read a book—or read of a book I should say—some years ago written by Frank Bullen. Frank Bullen said he had actually seen fish big enough to swallow a man. I never heard anyone attack Frank Bullen's works. I never read any articles written against Frank Bullen's writings. Frank Bullen wrote he had actually seen in the stomachs of whales whole fish twelve times larger than an average human body. I never heard anyone say, "Well, I don't believe what Frank Bullen said." But you let someone read out of the book of Jonah that a fish swallowed a man and he lived inside three days by a miracle of God and people will say, "I am not going to believe that old-fashioned, archaic story." Well, Jesus believed it. Matthew 12:39-41 says:

"But he answered and said unto them, An evil and adulterous generation seeketh after a sign; and there shall no sign be given to it, but the sign of the prophet Jonas: For as Jonas was three days and three nights in the whale's belly; so shall the Son of man be three days and three nights in the heart of the earth. The men of Nineveh shall rise in judgment with this generation, and shall condemn it: because they repented at the preaching of Jonas; and, behold, a greater than Jonas is here."

Now watch this. First of all, Jesus said there was a Jonah. Secondly, He said Jonah was swallowed by a whale. Thirdly, He said Jonah did preach to Nineveh and Nineveh did repent. And Jesus Christ put His hand on the book of

Jonah and said, "Jonah is a book that is inspired of God." When a man comes along and says, "I don't believe the book of Jonah," he is calling Jesus Christ a liar and I resent that and I will have my piece to say about it.

Jesus said the book of Jonah, all the prophets, all the Scriptures are inspired of God. Jesus often quoted from the Pentateuch, especially Deuteronomy.

You say, "Preacher, that takes care of the Old Testament, but what about the New Testament?" Jesus took care of that, too, thank God. Before Jesus went away, He talked so much about the coming of the Holy Spirit after He was gone. Speaking of the Holy Spirit, Jesus said in John 14:26, "...he shall teach you all things, and bring all things to your remembrance, whatsoever I have said unto you." In John 16: 13 again He said, "Howbeit when he, the Spirit of truth, is come, he will guide you into all truth: for he shall not speak of himself; but whatsoever he shall hear, that shall he speak: and he will shew you things to come." Jesus reached out before it was ever written and laid His hand upon the New Testament and said, "The New Testament is the inspired Book of God."

So I have this morning the testimony of Jesus Christ. All of this Bible from Genesis to Revelation is God's Book and is inspired. If the Bible is not true, Jesus was not honest. We know and say of some men today, "Well, now, he may have his faults, but whatever he says you can depend on." That used to be an expression down in the country where I was raised. A man may curse and he may have some other bad habits, but a lot of times people will say, "Well, I will tell you one thing about him, whatever he says you can depend on; whatever he says he'll do, he will do; whatever he says you can know that it is true."

Listen, whatever Jesus said is good enough for me. I must make my choice this morning between the testimony of Jesus Christ, and the testimony of higher criticism and someone who does not know the Author of this Book, and thus, does not believe it. I will take the Word of Jesus Christ any time, because whatever He says you can depend on. I believe the Bible is inspired because of the testimony of Jesus Christ.

"The writing was the writing of God."—Exod. 32:16.
"These are the true sayings of God."—Rev. 19:9.

2. I Believe in the Inspiration of the Bible Because of Its Testimony of Fulfilled Prophecy

I believe, in the second place—and I am leading to something and I hope you will pray that God will help us to get it in our hearts this morning—in the inspiration of the Bible because of its testimony of fulfilled prophecy. You see, three-fourths of the Bible is prophecy. Three-fourths of this Book is history prewritten. Three-fourths of that three-fourths has already accurately been fulfilled. I say it again: Three-fourths of this book is prophecy. Three-fourths has already accurately been fulfilled just exactly like God said it would be.

Isaiah 34:16 is a wonderful verse. I have read it a good many times and thought about it and meditated on it. "Seek ye out of the book of the Lord, and read: no one of these shall fail, none shall want her mate: for my mouth it hath commanded, and his spirit it hath gathered them." God said not one prophecy of this Book shall ever want its mate. That is, God says, "Seek ye out of the book of the Lord, and read: no one of these shall fail, none shall want her mate ...." There will be a fulfillment to every prophetical statement in the Bible.

Now I have had people say to me, "Well, I do not know for sure about that Book," and I have asked a lot of people, "How do you explain a Book that gave the course of nations, the history of races of people and wrote history before it ever took place?" I have never yet had an intelligent explanation of the Bible without miraculous inspiration of God. I have never yet had that argument refuted. I have never yet had one human being give an intelligent dissenting answer. If this is not God's Book, how do you explain that it predicts the future? I would like to give you an example.

Suppose this morning we darken this building until we cannot see our hand before our face. I place a target, a bullseye, back against the wall and line up ten men with bows and arrows against this platform. To further complicate it, I put a blindfold over every man so he can't see if it is light or dark. I say to those men, "I have put a target on that back wall, and I want you to shoot at that bullseye. You can't see your hand before your face. You are blindfolded in addition to that, but I want you to shoot at the target and see if you can hit it."

We sit in breathless stillness. We hear the quivering of the bow, then hear the swift passing of the arrow through the air, then we hear the thud. We turn on the lights and remove the blindfolds and back on that wall are ten quivering arrows in the very heart of the target.

You say, "Preacher, if that could happen, I would know beyond any doubt that back of the shooting of those ten arrows there was a mastermind and a miracle hand that guided them all."

When I read of hundreds of years ago the blessed Book saying this will come to pass and that will come to pass and God's Book hitting the target every time, I must admit that back of it all there is a Mastermind and a miracle hand that wrote this Book. "The writing was the writing of God" (Exod. 32:16).

I wish I had time this morning to deal with some of the prophecies that have already been fulfilled. Think this morning of the prophecies that are related to Jesus Christ— His coming into the world; being born of a virgin; His place of birth; the manner of His birth; the time of His birth. Think of the prophecies already fulfilled concerning His life on earth and the works that He wrought. Think of the prophecies written hundreds of years before He ever died, telling how He would die, with whom He would die, what he would say while dying. Think of the prophecies relating to the Jews.

The chaplain of King Gustavus Adolphus was asked the question, "Sir, in one word will you give me an irrefutable proof of the inspiration of the Bible?" To his king he answered, "Jew, Jew."

You cannot explain it any other way—the prophecies concerning the Jew scattered over all the face of the earth. Go back to the book of Genesis and you find an accurate description of what is going on in the land of Palestine. God's holy Word says that the descendents of Ishmael and the descendants of Isaac (the Arabs and the Jews) would dwell in the presence of each other and that there would be war between the two until the end of time. God's holy Word predicted that thousands of years ago.

How would you explain this morning that even the book of Daniel could tell you what would happen to nations like Greece and Rome and Babylon? How do you explain that? This old book says Babylon will never be inhabited again, but it will be the dwelling places of owls and jackals and animals. Go today seventy miles south of the city of Baghdad and out in the midst of those stones see the animals darting here and there, then listen to it in God's Word:

"And Babylon, the glory of kingdoms, the beauty of the Chaldees' excellency, shall be as when God overthrew Sodom and Gomorrah. It shall never be inhabited, neither shall it be dwelt in from generation to generation: neither shall the Arabian pitch tent there; neither shall the shepherds make their fold there. But wild beasts of the desert shall lie there; and their houses shall be full of doleful creatures; and owls shall dwell there, and satyrs shall dance there."—Isa. 13:19-21.

How do you explain this miracle Book that predicts the future hundreds of years before it ever takes place? How would you explain when one day in the city of Capernaum

Jesus said, "And thou, Capernaum, which art exalted unto heaven, shalt be brought down to hell" (Matt. 11:23)? Go today where Capernaum used to be and you will see only the stones and rubble of that forgotten city. It came to pass just exactly like Jesus said it would.

This week I read the book of Obadiah, the shortest book in the Old Testament. I have read Obadiah scores and scores of times and it never meant as much to me as it does now. The book of Obadiah has to do with a prophecy of the people called the Edomites. The Edomites are descendants of Esau. God says of the land of Edom and the Edomites, "There shall not be any remaining of the house of Esau; for the Lord hath spoken it" (Obadiah 18).

Now there is no such thing today as an Edomite. God said there will not be a descendant called an Edomite left of the house of Esau. The Edomites are of the descendants of Esau and there is no such nation, no such people. You cannot find a single one. The place where he lived is a city called Petra, cut out of solid rock, 708 feet high in the mountains and God said He would destroy this city until there would not be one man left in it. A year ago I walked among the ruins of Petra and looked high up where the houses were built, and where those people had said, "We dwell in the clift of these rocks, this impregnable fortress, and we will never be destroyed." All you could see were visitors, but not one single inhabitant. The Word of God has come to pass just exactly like God said it would.

I will give you another example. In Ezekiel, chapter 26, God spoke of the great city of Tyre—Tyrus, as it was called in Ezekiel, chapter 26. God said, "...I will also scrape her dust from her, and make her like the top of a rock" (Ezek. 26:4). Two hundred and forty years went by and old Tyre still stood on the seashore, a mighty city with its navy and its army, its thousands of people, yet God said, "...I will also scrape her dust from her, and make her like the top of a rock." He said He would destroy the city of Tyre and it would never be rebuilt again. Some 240 dusty years went by and when Alexander the Great came on the scene, he built a causeway half a mile long and nearly as wide, went into the city of Tyre and utterly destroyed it. If you could go to the city of Tyre, you could hardly find a stone where it used to be.

You see God's Word always comes to pass. Luke 16:17 says, "And it is easier for heaven and earth to pass, than one tittle of the law to fail." A tittle is a little straight line used in making the Hebrew and Greek letters. Jesus said, "And it is easier for heaven and earth to pass, than one tittle of the law to fail."

I do not often get shouting happy but I couldn't help but say, "Glory to God!" as I read this poem the other day:

> Almighty Lord, the sun shall fail,
> The moon forget her nightly tale,
>
> The deepest silence hush on high,
> And the radiant course of the sky,
>
> But fixed for everlasting years
> Unmoved amid the wreck of spheres,
>
> Thy Word shall shine in cloudless day
> When Heaven and earth shall pass away.

And I said, "Glory to God!" I thank God that when the mountains have crumbled to dust, this Book will still be standing.

"The writing was the writing of God."—Exod. 32:16.
"These are the true sayings of God."—Rev. 19:9.

3. I Believe in the Inspiration of the Bible Because of Its Indestructibility

Jesus said, "The scripture cannot be broken" (John 10:35). I believe in the inspiration of the Bible, in the third place, because of its indestructibility. There have been times in the history of the church when as many as two thousand copies of this Book have been piled in one huge pile and burned. Boats have been sunk to the bottom of the sea merely because they carried copies of the blessed Bible. But I Peter 1:25 says, "But the word of the Lord endureth for ever. And this is the word which by the gospel is preached unto you." Isaiah 40:8 says, "The grass withereth, the flower fadeth: but the word of our God shall stand for ever." Atheism couldn't destroy it. Rationalism has not been able to do away with it. Higher criticism has fallen back in defeat. Science, falsely so-called, has accused it, but the old Bible still stands.

It reminds me of an Irishman a neighbor hired to build a fence. The neighbor told the Irishman, "I want it four feet high. I want you to not only guarantee me that it will be four feet high, but I want you to guarantee me that it will never fall."

The Irishman thought for a minute. "Now to build it four feet high wouldn't be so bad, but to guarantee that it will never fall will take some thinking."

So the Irishman thought a few days, then he built it. When he got all through and ready to collect, the neighbor said, "Is it four feet high?"

"Yes, it is four feet high."

"What assurance do I have that it will not fall down?"

The Irishman said, "Well, I not only built it four feet high, but I built it five feet thick, so if it falls down it will be a foot higher than it was before it fell."

I think of that when I think of the Bible. Thank God, every attack against it only lifts it up a little more and makes people know it is more secure than the Rock of Gibraltar. Every time it is attacked, it rises a thousand feet higher as the best seller of all the ages and the miracle Book of God! There is a poem which says:

> Hammer away ye rebel bands
> Your hammers break, God's Anvil stands.

Last eve I paused beside the blacksmith's door,
  And heard the anvil ring the vesper chime;
Then looking in, I saw upon the floor
  Old hammers worn with beating years of time.

"How many anvils have you had," said I,
  "To wear and batter all these hammers so?"
"Just one," said he, and then with twinkling eye,
  "The anvil wears the hammers out, you know."

"And so," I thought, "the Anvil of God's Word
  For ages skeptic blows have beat upon,
Yet, though the noise of falling blows was heard,
  The Anvil is unharmed, the hammers gone."

You see, God's Book is an indestructible Book. If today by some insidious plan of the Devil, every copy of this Book could be eliminated from the earth (it has been translated in over a thousand languages), you could get a group of Christians together and write every word of it again because it is in the hearts of God's people. It is an indestructible Book. It is an integral part of people who are saved. I believe in the inspiration of the Bible.

"The writing was the writing of God."—Exod. 32:16.
"These are the true sayings of God."—Rev. 19:9.

4. I Believe in the Inspiration of the Bible Because of Its Unparalled Unity

I believe, in the fourth place, in the inspiration of the Bible because of its unparalleled unity. There are no mistakes in it, no contradictions in it. Sixty-six books, forty human writers, written over a period of fifteen hundred years, on more than one continent and written in three different languages, and when you put it together it has one harmonious theme, the blood of Jesus Christ, and not one contradiction in it.

I read a little humorous thing one time. A man thought

he had found a contradiction in Proverbs 26:4,5: "Answer not a fool according to his folly," and "Answer a fool according to his folly." The man said to the Christian, "Look there! The Bible says, 'Answer not a fool according to his folly' and then it says, 'Answer a fool according to his folly.'" But the Christian wouldn't talk to him. He just kept ignoring the man, kept silent. The man kept on, so finally the Christian put him in his place. He said, "You see, there are no contradictions in the Bible. It said one place, 'Answer not a fool according to his folly' and the very next verse says, 'Answer a fool according to his folly.' And that is exactly what has just happened in this conversation. So you see, there are no contradictions in it."

Look magazine has gotten to be as dirty as *Playboy* and *Esquire*. It is almost too filthy to come into the homes of decent people. The magazines Christians could subscribe to ten years ago are now so vulgar you would be ashamed to have the mailman put them in your mailbox. *Look* magazine several years ago came out with an article entitled, "Fifty Thousand Errors in the Bible." I thought, Now I am not smart, I am just a country preacher, but I know that that is not true. I am going to lift my voice. So I wrote letter after letter to the editor of *Look* magazine. I asked him to name one, prove one, substantiate one. I answered some of the things he had written in his article, so twisted and distorted. I never so much as got a letter. I am telling you this morning, here is a Book with no errors in it!

I never will forget a boy Mrs. Malone and I picked up on the highway one time. When asked, "Are you a Christian?" he said, "No, I'm not, but I would be if there weren't so many contradictions in the Bible."

I said, "Who told you there were contradictions in the Bible?"

"My preacher."

"Did he show them to you?"

"Yeah, he showed me lots of them."

I said, "You know that to be true now?"

"Yeah, I know that to be true. There are a lot of contradictions in the Bible."

I said, "And you know where they are?"

He said, "Yes, sir, I know exactly where they are. He pointed them out to me."

I said, "If a fellow wanted you to point them out to him, could you do it?"

"Oh, yes."

I reached over and touched the button on the glove compartment, the door fell down and a Bible almost jumped out on his lap. I handed it to the boy and said, "You know, I am a preacher and a Christian. I am going to hold a revival meeting in the thumb part of Michigan. I would like to find out about some of those contradictions before I go up there and preach to those people."

He took that Bible, he looked at it as if he had never seen one before. He turned it every way you could turn it. He turned it over and over and looked at me and looked at the Bible. He said, "Well, a...well now...a...well now let me see, a...well...I tell you this much, if my preacher was here, he could show them to you."

I said, "No, Son, he couldn't show them to me any more than you can show me."

There are none! God never contradicts His Word. He has written a perfect Book, a glorious, perfect revelation of Jesus Christ and His power to save.

"The writing was the writing of God."—Exod. 32:16.
"These are the true sayings of God."—Rev. 19:9.

5. I Believe in the Inspiration of the Bible Because of the Testimony of Its Transforming Power

Again, let me say, I believe in the inspiration of the Bible because of the testimony of its transforming power. Oh, I wish I had the time to talk to you about the transforming power, the life-changing power of the Bible. Jesus said in

John 5:24, "Verily, verily, I say unto you, He that heareth my word, and believeth on him that sent me, hath everlasting life, and shall not come into condemnation; but is passed from death unto life." Romans 10:17 says, "So then faith cometh by hearing, and hearing by the word of God." First Peter 1:23 says, "Being born again, not of corruptible seed, but of incorruptible, by the word of God, which liveth and abideth for ever." I believe that this is God's Book because of its transforming power.

When that great Christian, Sir Walter Scott, was dying, he said to a nephew, "Bring me the Book." There were thousands of books in his library. The nephew said, "Uncle Walter, which book?" Walter Scott answered, "There is but one Book; bring me the Bible."

That is the way I feel this morning. I feel like Paul who said in the letter to the Romans, "Let God be true, but every man a liar" (Rom. 3:4). I believe in the inspiration of the Bible!

When Lord Kelvin, that great English scientist, was asked, "What is your greatest discovery?" he said, "My greatest discovery is a truth in the Bible that Christ Jesus came into the world to save sinners, of whom I am chief."

Two beautiful little verses of a wonderful poem about the Bible:

> Thou truest Friend man ever knew,
>   Thy constancy I have tried.
> When all were false, I found thee true
>   My Counsellor and my Guide.
>
> The mines of earth no treasure give
>   That can this volume buy.
> In teaching me the way to live
>   It taught me how to die.

I believe in the Bible.

"The writing was the writing of God."—Exod. 32:16.

"These are the true sayings of God."—Rev. 19:9.

6. I Believe in the Inspiration of the Bible Because of Its Inexhaustibility

This Bible transcends the mind of natural man because it contains the mind of God. Its treasures are never all discovered by any single intellect. Its depths are immeasurable, its heights reach far beyond the highest pinnacle of human discernment. Even the brilliant and logical mind of a great Christian genius like Paul must fall back in breathless admiration. Romans 11:33 and 34 says, "O the depth of the riches both of the wisdom and knowledge of God! how unsearchable are his judgments, and his ways past finding out! For who hath known the mind of the Lord? or who hath been his counsellor?"

The Prophet Isaiah paid an eternal tribute to the inexhaustibility of the Word of God. Read it in Isaiah 55:8 and 9 which says, "For my thoughts are not your thoughts, neither are your ways my ways, saith the Lord. For as the heavens are higher than the earth, so are my ways higher than your ways, and my thoughts than your thoughts."

Dr. R. A. Torrey once said:

> Many men of strongest intellect, of marvelous power of penetration, of broadest culture, have given a lifetime to the study of the Bible; and no man who has really studied it has ever dreamed of saying that he has gotten to the bottom of the Book. New light is constantly breaking forth from the Word of God. The fact that it has proved itself unfathomable for these centuries is positive proof that in it are hidden the infinite treasures of the wisdom of God.

The deeper you search into this mine of blessed truth, richer and deeper and wider and more precious becomes the vein of priceless gems. It is like a perennial spring, a summitless mountain, a bottomless ocean, an endless song. It is a gallery of never-ending rooms! Thank God for this light in darkness, this balm for our wounds, this anchor for our souls.

"The writing was the writing of God."—Exod 32:16.
"These are the true sayings of God."—Rev. 19:9.

7. I Believe in the Inspiration of the Bible Because of an Inward Witness

In I Corinthians 2:14 we read, "But the natural man receiveth not the things of the Spirit of God: for they are foolishness unto him: neither can he know them, because they are spiritually discerned." Now I know that higher criticism, pseudoscience, and unregenerate scholarship may scoff at this as a proof of inspiration, but mocking and ridicule does not disprove anything. The child of God has an inward witness about many things: assurance of salvation, hope for the future and certainty about this Book of God. Just as the Holy Spirit is the Author of the Bible, He is also the Tenant of my body. As I read what He wrote, inwardly He assures me of its authenticity and reliability.

My heart tells me even as my head does that this is God's Word. If one wants proof of this inward witness, he should carefully study I Corinthians 2:10-13 which says:

"But God hath revealed them unto us by his Spirit: for the Spirit searcheth all things, yea, the deep things of God. For what man knoweth the things of a man, save the spirit of man which is in him? even so the things of God knoweth no man, but the Spirit of God. Now we have received, not the spirit of the world, but the spirit which is of God; that we might know the things that are freely given to us of God. Which things also we speak, not in the words which man's wisdom teacheth, but which the Holy Ghost teacheth; comparing spiritual things with spiritual."

This passage already clearly teaches that the Holy Spirit who indwells every believer, testifies that the blessed Holy Bible is the teaching, "which the Holy Ghost teacheth." My heart tells me that the Bible is inspired of God.

I have read this Book in the deepest valley of sorrow and the Spirit said, "This is My Word." I have read it in the midst of trouble and in the darkest night of frustration and the Spirit seemed to say, "This is My Word." I have read it with tears, read it with joy, read it with unanswered question and always the same witness, "This is My Word." I have read it when some mocked, some laughed, others doubted. I have read it when demons seemed to scream against it, multitudes paid no attention to it, but always the same inward witness, "This is My Word." I have read it in moments of triumph and victory when it seemed that angels shouted, "This is the Book of God."

I rejoice in the inward testimony that this is the Word of God.

"The writing was the writing of God."—Exod. 32:16.
"These are the true sayings of God."—Rev. 19:9.

Do you know the Author of this Book? Are you acquainted with Him whose face is stamped on every page and whose atoning blood stains every syllable? He is the Saviour of those who believe in Him. May God help you to turn to Him and trust Him.

THE VIRGIN BIRTH OF JESUS CHRIST

or

WHY JESUS BECAME A MAN

"Christ Jesus: Who, being in the form of God, thought it not robbery to be equal with God: But made himself of no reputation, and took upon him the form of a servant, and was made in the likeness of men: And being found in fashion as a man, he humbled himself, and became obedient unto death, even the death of the cross."—Phil. 2:5-8.

I. He Became a Man That He Might Subject Himself to the Limitations of the Human Body

II. He Became a Man That He Might Subject Himself to Man's Sins

III. He Became a Man That He Might Subject Himself to Man's Death and the Grave

IV. He Became a Man That He Might Subject Himself As a Man to Adam's Curse

V. He Became a Man That We Might Be Made in the Likeness of God

Shepherds' Field near Bethlehem

"And the angel said unto them, Fear not....For unto you is born this day in the city of David a Saviour, which is Christ the Lord."—Luke 2:10,11.

2

The Virgin Birth of Jesus Christ

or
Why Jesus Became a Man

"Christ Jesus: Who, being in the form of God, thought it not robbery to be equal with God: But made himself of no reputation, and took upon him the form of a servant, and was made in the likeness of men: And being found in fashion as a man, he humbled himself, and became obedient unto death, even the death of the cross."—Phil. 2:5-8.

I would like to speak to you on the incarnation of Christ. The subject is, "Jesus in the Likeness of Men" or "Why Jesus Became a Man." There are two phrases in this passage that I call to your attention. Philippians 2:7 and 8 have these two expressions: *"made in the likeness of men"* and *"being found in fashion as a man."* And that is the subject, "Why Jesus Became a Man."

Someone may want to distinguish between the virgin birth of Jesus and the incarnation of Jesus. In a sense there is a difference, yet these two subjects are closely related. The virgin birth involves that miraculous act of God whereby the Lord Jesus was conceived, without man, in the body of a pure virgin maiden named Mary. The incarnation is the divine act of God whereby Jesus was manifest in human flesh.

Many passages speak of the virgin birth. Matthew 1:18-20 says:

"Now the birth of Jesus Christ was on this wise: When as his mother Mary was espoused to Joseph, before they came together, she was found with child of the Holy Ghost. Then

Joseph her husband, being a just man, and not willing to make her a publick example, was minded to put her away privily. But while he thought on these things, behold, the angel of the Lord appeared unto him in a dream, saying, Joseph, thou son of David, fear not to take unto thee Mary thy wife: for that which is conceived in her is of the Holy Ghost."

Other passages such as those in our text deal specifically with the incarnation of Jesus. John 1:14 says:

"And the Word was made flesh, and dwelt among us, (and we beheld his glory, the glory as of the only begotten of the Father,) full of grace and truth."

First Timothy 3:16 says:

"And without controversy great is the mystery of godliness: God was manifest in the flesh, justified in the Spirit, seen of angels, preached unto the Gentiles, believed on in the world, received up into glory."

If one attacks the virgin birth of our Lord, he also attacks the incarnation of Jesus. In recent years especially, there has been a blatant, insidious attack by rationalists, modernists and infidels against the virgin birth and incarnation of Jesus. For instance, there are some who say that the word *virgin* as found in the English translation of the Bible does not necessarily mean a chaste, pure, young woman. Some contend that the Hebrew word *almah* does not mean virgin, but young woman, that is, any kind of young woman. This is not true.

Let us examine Isaiah 7:14 which says, "Therefore the Lord himself shall give you a sign; Behold, a virgin shall conceive and bear a son, and shall call his name Immanuel." The word *virgin* here definitely means a pure, chaste woman who has not known man. This is its meaning in Genesis 24:43 when Rebekah is called a virgin; this is its meaning in Proverbs 30:19 and also in Psalm 68:25. In Matthew 1:23

God quotes Isaiah 7:14 and in the Greek New Testament says *virgin.*

The birth mentioned in Isaiah 7:14 was to be a miraculous sign to the house of David and to all the world. How could the natural birth of a baby boy be a special sign? Hasn't this happened millions of times? No, in order to be a sign it must be a birth by a virgin who had not known man.

There are three general names of Jesus many, many times in the Bible. For instance, you find Jesus spoken of as the Son of David, Son of God and Son of Man. The Son of David is His Jewish name, His racial name. All of us know that nearly every book in the Bible was written by a Jew. Jesus came from the tribe of Judah, the family of David, and He was a Jew.

Then there is the Son of God. This is His divine name.

But there is another name. I wonder if we study it as much as we ought to. Jesus is called the "Son of Man." Eighty times in the Word of God, Jesus Christ is spoken of as the Son of Man.

We'll look at some of the verses where Jesus is spoken of as the Son of Man in a minute. But what I want you to think of is Jesus Christ, as a Man—Jesus Christ in a human body. Yes, a body just like your body and my body. Jesus was perfect. Jesus was divine. But Jesus had a human body.

Now many times in the Bible Jesus is called a Man. The Son of God is called a Man. He was called a human being. We read, for instance, in Hebrews 2:14, "Forasmuch then as the children are partakers of flesh and blood, he also himself likewise took part of the same...." Now here in the Word of God it plainly and simply declares that Jesus Christ took part of "flesh and blood." Don't forget that. I believe that the humanity of Jesus is of vast importance. I've heard great scholars and Bible teachers say that the humanity of Jesus needed to be emphasized in our preaching and teaching just as much as the deity of Jesus.

The woman at the well who got gloriously saved, went

back into the city and said, "A man, which told me all things that ever I did" (John 4:29).

When she viewed Jesus sitting on the well there in Samaria, she looked on Him and recognized God to be in the form of a man. Jesus spoke of Himself as having flesh and blood on many occasions. In John 6:53 and 54 Jesus said, "Except ye eat the flesh of the Son of man, and drink his blood, ye have no life in you. Whoso eateth my flesh, and drinketh my blood, hath eternal life...." So Jesus claimed that He was a Man. Jesus claimed that He had flesh and blood.

Many, many times, in connection with all the great things that He did, Jesus referred to Himself as the Son of Man. When He was talking to Nicodemus that night, in John, chapter 3, He said, "And as Moses lifted up the serpent in the wilderness, even so must the Son of man be lifted up: That whosoever believeth in him should not perish, but have eternal life" (vss. 14, 15). When Jesus talked of Calvary, redemption, the cross and the shedding of His blood for the salvation of the world, He referred to Himself as the Son of Man.

Notice it again in Luke 19:10. He had just saved Zacchaeus and people wondered that He was such a wonderful friend of sinners. Jesus said, "For the Son of man is come to seek and to save that which was lost" (Luke 19:10). So we see His humanity connected with His divine purpose in coming into the world.

Notice again, Jesus spoke of Himself as the Son of Man when He spoke of the resurrection. "For as Jonas was three days and three nights in the whale's belly; so shall the Son of man be three days and three nights in the heart of the earth" (Matt. 12:40).

Notice also when Jesus spoke of the Second Coming, He spoke of Himself as being the Son of Man: "But as the days of Noe were, so shall also the coming of the Son of man be .... For in such an hour as ye think not the Son of man cometh" (Matt. 24:37, 44).

Lest you think that I am emphasizing something that Jesus did not emphasize; lest you think that this preacher is emphasizing something the Word of God does not emphasize, let me tell you, no less than eighty times Jesus Christ was referred to in the Bible as the Son of Man. Son of God, yes, but Son of Man just as surely and distinctively; so the Bible declares.

Now you say, "Why is that important?" I want to give you in a moment five Bible reasons why it was important for Jesus to become a Man to be our Saviour.

You think of the humanity of Jesus and what it all means to us as believers. I think of the story of a certain little girl. It is said that one stormy night a little girl in her bedroom began to cry. She was afraid of the thunder, lightning, wind, and the rain. The mother went up and tried to comfort her. "Now honey, you are not alone. You know God is in our hearts, and in our home." Mother said, "The Lord is with you." When she started to leave the room, the little girl continued to weep. Finally the mother went back to the bed and the little girl said, "I know the Lord is with me, but Mother, I want somebody with skin on." In other words, she was saying, "I want someone I can feel and touch; someone I can see."

That, my friends, is exactly what Jesus did. He came in visible form. He humbled Himself and lived on earth in the fashion of a Man.

You say to me, "Why was it necessary for Jesus Christ, the Son of God, the member of the Trinity, from the very beginning, the preexistent, the eternally existing Son of God —why must He become a Man?"

I believe there are five great Bible reasons.

I. He Became a Man That He Might Subject Himself to the Limitations of the Human Body

Did you ever think of the body of Jesus and all the limitations of the human body?

First, He subjected Himself to childlike obedience to His parents. You just think of that little Babe born in a manger that night; that little Babe snuggled in a mother's arms; that little Baby nursing from a mother's breast; that little Baby carried about, taken care of, and cleansed. That little Baby in human form is Almighty God. See Him at the age of twelve, as recorded in the book of Luke. When His parents journeyed homeward, they missed Him and came back to the Temple and found Him.

He said, 'What, know you not that I must be about my Father's business?' Then they went on their way home and you read this of Jesus—twelve years of age, the blessed Son of God, in the body of a little Boy, "And he went down with them, and came to Nazareth, and was subject unto them" (Luke 2:51). Jesus Christ subjected Himself to childlike obedience. He minded His parents. He honored His mother and father. He subjected Himself to all the limitations of a human body.

Jesus knew what it was to be subject to fatigue. The Son of God who made all things that are made, yet became tired. That body became worn and tired with many long hours of labor.

I read a beautiful thing in Mark 4. One day amidst a storm, Jesus was on the boat. The storm was arising and the disciples came. And we read in Mark 4:38 that Jesus "was in the hinder part of the ship, asleep on a pillow" and they awake Him. The Son of God got so tired from toiling, laboring, ministering, speaking, loving and weeping over people that His body became worn out, He became tired and sleepy, so He lay on the deck of a vessel on a borrowed pillow. He had to be awakened even in the midst of a storm. The body of Jesus was subject to fatigue.

The body of Jesus was subject to hunger. Jesus knew what it was to want food, to be hungry, to look for something to eat. He looked upon the fig tree. Mark 11:12 says, "And on the morrow, when they were come from Bethany, he was hungry." When you think of Jesus, don't always think of Him working a miracle to meet His needs. Think of Him as being in a human body, subject to limitations such as you and I are. Jesus was hungry.

Jesus subjected Himself not only to childlike obedience, fatigue, and hunger, but He subjected Himself to thirst. The body of Jesus knew what it was to crave water. See Him as a Stranger sitting on a well in that hot noontime of the day saying to a woman, "Give me to drink," recorded in John 4:7. Just that plain, simple statement, "Give me to drink"—Jesus was thirsty. Jesus perspired. Jesus got dusty. Jesus walked along the road. He wanted water. He begged for something to drink. Jesus subjected His body to human limitations. And almost the last thing He said on the cross was, "I thirst." That body knew fever and pain and suffering, and wanted water. It was a human body.

See it again. His body was subjected to limitations.

Jesus' body was subjected to deprivation. Jesus knew what it was to want some things that He didn't have because He came in the form of a man to walk among men. Listen to Him; one time He said, "The foxes have holes, and the birds of the air have nests; but the Son of man hath not where to lay his head" (Matt. 8:20). Jesus was deprived. He owned no home. Read John 7:53 and 8:1, "And every man went unto his own house...Jesus went unto the mount of Olives." When others said, "I'm going home," Jesus said, "I'll go to the garden and pray." "I'll go to the mountain and pray." He had no home of His own. "The foxes have holes, and the birds of the air have nests; but the Son of man hath not where to lay his head" (Matt. 8:20). Jesus Christ was subjected to all the limitations of the human body. Oh, how I thank God for that!

You know the Bible says He "was in all points tempted like as we are, yet without sin" (Heb. 4:15). And the Word of God says, "For in that he himself hath suffered being tempted, he is able to succour them that are tempted" (Heb.

2:18). When you are thirsty and tired, hungry and deprived, remember, Jesus in a human body went through all that. So first of all He subjected Himself to the limitations of a human body. Oh, He gave Himself in a body.

I think of it so often on the first Sunday of the month when we observe the Lord's Supper, the ordinance of communion. I think of the statement in I Corinthians 11:24 where Paul quotes Jesus, "...Take, eat: this is my body, which is broken for you...." The word "broken" is inserted. It should read, "...Take, eat: this is my body, which is for you...." He said, "My body is for you." Jesus took upon Himself a body. Why? For you! That was God's way for Christ to be revealed and manifested in a human body, subject to all the limitations of a human body.

'He was made in the likeness of men.'—Phil. 2:8.

II. He Became a Man that He Might Subject Himself to Man's Sins

The Bible plainly teaches that Jesus became a Man that He might assume the penalty of man's sin. Notice what the penalty is in the Bible. Romans 6:23, "The wages of sin is death...." That is the penalty for sin. The Bible plainly teaches, "The soul that sinneth, it shall die" (Ezek. 18:4, 20). You and I have sinned. "The wages of sin is death...." The penalty is death, spiritual death, to be cut off from God. In I Corinthians 15:3 we read this statement, "...Christ died for our sins according to the scriptures." I read in II Corinthians more about Jesus being subjected to man's sin. "For he [God] hath made him [Jesus] to be sin for us, who knew no sin; that we might be made the righteousness of God in him" (II Cor. 5:21). God made Him a Sin-offering. God made Him in the form of a Man that we might be made the righteousness of God in Him. Have you ever wondered, Did Jesus as a Man ever identify Himself with our sins?

Listen to Him on the cross. I read something about this wonderful statement recently that I had never seen before in the Word of God, and that is the statement of Jesus recorded in Matthew 27:46 where, dying on the cross midst the darkness, Jesus cried, "My God, my God, why hast thou forsaken me?" Oh, how many times have I read it! How many times have I repeated it! How many times has it gone through my mind! That statement of Jesus, "My God, my God...." Jesus never called His Father that before. He always said, "My Father." "I and my Father are one." "He that hath seen me hath seen the Father." "I do always those things that please him [the Father]." But here He is on the cross and He cries, "My God, my God, why hast thou forsaken me?"

Did you ever wonder why? Psalm 22 answers the question of Jesus, "My God, my God, why hast thou forsaken me? why art thou so far from helping me, and from the words of my roaring? O my God, I cry in the daytime [that is when it is light], but thou hearest not; and in the night season [that is when it was dark hanging on that cross], and am not silent." Now the Word of God answers the question that Jesus asked, in Psalm 22:3, "But thou art holy, O thou that inhabitest the praises of Israel." Hear it! That is why God turned His face away when Jesus became a Sin-offering on the cross. The book of Habakkuk says, "Thou art of purer eyes than to behold evil, and canst not look on iniquity" (Hab. 1:13). And when Jesus was identified with your sin and mine, God the Father turned His face away. No wonder yonder sun refused to shine. No wonder the blessed Saviour cried, "My God, my God, why hast thou forsaken me?" Your sin and mine were upon Him, in that crucial hour when the Son of Man was lifted up that He might redeem us from all iniquity.

Oh, listen, He became a Man that He might subject Himself to man's sin, and the penalty of man's sin. Oh, what Isaiah 53 has to say! That mountain peak of Bible prophecy! That great chapter of the Gospel in the book of Isaiah! Old Testament Gospel, Isaiah 53—I like to think of it. I think some twenty-four times in Isaiah 53 we are shown Another taking our place. Forty-eight times there are personal pronouns used in these twelve verses. Listen to what it says about Jesus.

"Who hath believed our report? and to whom is the arm of the Lord revealed? [Jesus is the Arm of the Lord to do His bidding, to execute His will, to accomplish His work.] *For he shall grow up before him as a tender plant, and as a root out of a dry ground: he hath no form nor comeliness; and when we shall see him, there is no beauty that we should desire him. He is despised and rejected of men; a man of sorrows, and acquainted with grief: and we hid as it were our faces from him; he was despised, and we esteemed him not. Surely he hath borne our griefs, and carried our sorrows: yet we did esteem him stricken, smitten of God, and afflicted. But he was wounded for our transgressions, he was bruised for our iniquities: the chastisement of our peace was upon him; and with his stripes we are healed. All we like sheep have gone astray; we have turned every one to his own way; and the Lord hath laid on him the iniquity of us all."—Isa. 53:1-6.*

Yes, Jesus was in the form of Man that He might subject Himself to man's sin.

Dr. Harry Ironside was a great Bible teacher, and always in his interpretation of the Bible he led to Christ. Everything he said pointed to Jesus, always explaining what Jesus did and who He was and what He came to do.

Dr. Harry Ironside told one time of a sheep ranch that he visited down in Texas. He said he saw one of the greatest demonstrations of the righteousness of God imputed to us because Jesus, as a Man, died on the cross. He said He saw something he couldn't figure out. It looked like a sheep with four front legs and four back legs and two heads. It looked like a deformity. It looked like an abnormal little animal.

He asked the sheep rancher, "What in the world is this?"

The rancher smiled and said, "Preacher, this is probably a story that you will tell the rest of your life. We had a little lamb to die and a mother sheep died. The lamb left a mother without a baby and a mother died which left the lamb without a mother. We took the little lamb without a mother and put it in the pen of the mother without its baby. The mother didn't want the baby. She didn't want any part of it. She would lower her head and push it away.

"Some of the help here got the idea that if the mother thought that that little lamb was really hers, she would adopt it and make it as her own. She would nurse it and raise it and that would solve the whole problem. So they took the skin off the little dead lamb and put it around the little orphan lamb. We tied it on and that is why you see four front feet, four back feet and what looks like two heads.

"When it was covered we put it in the pen with the mother and she loved it and cared for it. There is nothing horrible about it to her. It is beautiful to her. She has accepted it because it is clothed in the garments of her own."

Old Dr. Ironside said, "What a perfect illustration of orphan sinners with no Father and no Saviour. But robed in the righteousness of God we are accepted in the beloved." That is the result of Jesus becoming a Man and identifying Himself with man's sins.

"...that we might be made the righteousness of God in him."—II Cor. 5:21.

'He was made in the likeness of men.'—Phil. 2:8.

III. He Became a Man That He Might Subject Himself to Man's Death and the Grave

All men, save one generation of Christians who live when Jesus comes, are subject unto death. From the first family, Adam and Eve, to this hour none have escaped the great reaper of Death. The Word of God tells us many times about man being subject to death. We don't get very far in the book of Genesis until some eight times we read "...and he died...and he died...and he died" (Gen. 5). Some men lived nearly a thousand years. But this is the summary of his life: "And he died...and he died." The Bible teaches us that all men are subject to death.

I hope He doesn't and I don't expect Him to, but if Jesus should tarry, every man, every woman, every boy, and every girl must walk across the chilly waters of Jordan. We must cross from time to eternity, and out of the land of the living into eternity. Every one of us must. Even Jesus went to the grave.

I read of a good man who lived in a town not too far from Jerusalem, a little town called Arimathaea. His name was Joseph. He is spoken of in the Bible as Joseph of Arimathaea. I read this: "This man went unto Pilate, and begged the body of Jesus. And he took it down, and wrapped it in linen, and laid it in a sepulchre that was hewn in stone, wherein never man before was laid" (Luke 23:52,53). Oh, what a picture! Here is a man who one day hewed out of the side of a rock a great tomb. He said to his family, "Here are graves for two adults and one child. Here is our family plot. When I go, this is where I will be buried, this will be my grave." But oh, the substitutionary love of God and Christ is seen on nearly every page of the Bible, and here it is. Not Joseph of Arimathaea was laid in that grave but the human body of the Son of God was in that grave—and wrapped in linen clothes. A huge stone closed the door and sealed it off. His enemies stood there and said, "We will see that forever He is a victim of the grave. We will see that that body of flesh and blood will rot in this soil because death has Him now!" They were wrong, but Jesus Christ was made in the likeness of men so He might subject Himself to man's grave.

Isaiah 53:9 says, "And he made his grave with the wicked, and with the rich in his death...." "With the wicked"—that is between the two thieves on the cross. "With the rich"— that is Joseph and Nicodemus, who begged His body and buried Him. He made His grave. Listen, it is seven hundred years before Jesus ever came in Bethlehem's manger.

The Word of God says, "He is to have a grave. He is to know what it means to be buried. He is to know, like all men know, what it is to die in a human body. He is to taste and experience death. That is why He became a Man."

Oh, when I think of death and the victory God has given those who believe on Him, I feel like Paul in I Corinthians 15. Here you see the resurrection of believers and of Christ discussed from five different views. I hear Paul in I Corinthians 15:55. I don't think that he ever gave a more wonderful shout of victory than he did in that chapter when he said, "O death, where is thy sting? O grave, where is thy victory?" Then he went on to say that Christ has taken the sting out of death and taken victory from the grasp of the grave. Why? Because He became a Man and died like all men will have to do if Jesus tarries.

I thank God there has been One to the grave before me, One whom I love, One who loves me with an eternal, unbounding, everlasting love. He has walked that way and left a light in the tomb for me when I go that way. Oh, He was made a Man that He might know what it means to die.

Did you ever hear of this sweet story of a little girl and mother? They were picking flowers and a bee came around. The little girl became alarmed as the bee was getting closer and buzzing around. She said, "Mother, I am afraid of the bee." She stayed close to her mother and in a moment she said again, "Mother, I am afraid that the bee will sting me."

The mother in a moment said, "No, honey, that bee will never sting you."

The little girl said, "Why do you say that? How do you know that bee is not going to sting me?"

As the mother scratched at the swollen place in her arm to find the stinger, she said, "Because it has already stung me. There is the stinger in Mother's arm. That bee will never harm you now."

And when I hear Paul cry, "O death, where is thy sting?

O grave, where is thy victory?" I thank God I can say, "In the body, the human body of the Son of God is the sting."

When the Christian dies it is a triumph. It is a moving to a glorious land, the land where living waters flow. It is a change of address. It is moving out of an old tent which rots and decays, into a house eternal not made with hands prepared for those who love the Lord. So He became a Man that He might be subject unto man's death and the grave.

'He was made in the likeness of men.'—Phil. 2:8.

IV. He Became a Man That He Might Subject Himself As a Man to Adam's Curse

Constantly in the Bible there is a comparison drawn. Had I the time, I would like to talk to you about what it meant when He said He "thought it not robbery to be equal with God." You know how Adam wanted to be equal with God? When the Devil said to him, "If you eat of that tree of the knowledge of good and evil and the forbidden fruit, you shall not die, as God said, but you shall be as God knowing good and evil" (Gen. 3). The first Adam sought to be like God by robbery. Jesus "thought it not robbery to be equal with God." He *was* equal with God. He sought to prove His deity by obedience, not robbery. And in obedience He came in the fashion of a Man and humbled Himself, even unto the death of the cross. But He subjected Himself to Adam's curse. I am amazed when I read about the curse God pronounced—a fourfold curse on the woman, on the man, on the serpent, and on the earth.

We are children of Adam and Jesus took upon Himself Adam's curse. I read where God said to Adam in Genesis 3:17 and 18, "...cursed is the ground for thy sake...Thorns also and thistles shall it bring forth...." Read it again, the curse of Adam is thorns. Read in the book of Matthew 27:29, "And when they had platted a crown of thorns, they put it upon his head, and a reed in his right hand: and they bowed the knee before him, and mocked him...." I have always known that that crown of thorns represented the thorns in Adam's curse. But what about that reed? Remember God said to Adam in Genesis 3:18, "Thou shalt eat the herb of the field."—'Out among the grass and weeds and herbs of the field, you will wring your living from the soil, by the sweat of your brow.' There is a crown of thorns on His head. There is a reed in His hand and man mocking the Son of God. That is what Paul wrote to the Galatians about when he said, "Christ hath redeemed us from the curse of the law, being made a curse for us: for it is written, Cursed is every one that hangeth on a tree" (Gal. 3:13).

I was talking to Mrs. Malone about a song that I have thought so much of in recent days. Just part of it would come to me. The song starts like this:

> I saw One hanging on a tree
> In agony and blood.
> He fixed His languid eyes on me,
> As near His cross I stood.

And a chorus says:

> He's looking on you!
> He's looking on you!
> O ever were love and compassion
> Love and compassion so true.
> He's looking on you!
> He's looking on you!
> He's looking, looking on you!

Another verse to the first song says:

> A second look He gave, which said,
> "I freely all forgive:
> This blood is for thy ransom paid,
> I die that thou may'st live."

Thank God, the curse is gone. It is gone! It is removed. It is lifted, to those who believe.

Yes, He subjected Himself to the body of a Man that He might assume man's curse.

'He was made in the likeness of men.'—Phil. 2:8.

V. He Became a Man That We Might Be Made in the Likeness of God

Oh, what beautiful truth! Oh, what a beautiful story! He was made like man that we may be made like God. How often it is taught in the Bible. First John 3:1-3 says:

"Behold, what manner of love the Father hath bestowed upon us, that we should be called the sons of God: therefore the world knoweth us not, because it knew him not. Beloved, now are we the sons of God, and it doth not yet appear what we shall be: but we know that, when he shall appear, we shall be like him; for we shall see him as he is."

Romans 8:29 declares the whole purpose of this salvation story: "For whom he did foreknow, he also did predestinate to be conformed to the image of his Son...." Oh, that is what it is all about! You know, I've heard folks argue that some are predestinated to go to Heaven and some are predestinated to be lost. But neither one of those things is true. Certainly no one is predestinated to be lost, for God loves the whole world. The Bible never teaches any such thing as a person elected or predestinated to go to Heaven. Election and predestination are not to go to Heaven. Those who are saved are predestinated and foreordained to be like Christ. That is what it is, wherever you read of it in the Bible. "For whom he did foreknow, he also did predestinate to be conformed to the image of his Son" (Rom. 8:29).

"...when he shall appear, we shall be like him." Oh, I like that! That is what I want. I've tried for these thirty-one years to grow more like Him and I've failed so many times. What a sweet truth it is to my needy heart! When the Lord comes I'm going to be like Him in full redemption, not only in soul but in body. I'm going to be like the Master.

First Corinthians 15:49 says, speaking of the first Adam, "And as we have borne the image of the earthy, we shall also bear the image of the heavenly." We are going to be like Jesus. The psalmist of old said, "I shall be satisfied, when I awake, with thy likeness" (Ps. 17:15). Many times in the Bible this beautiful truth is taught. For instance, see Philippians 3. He was made in the likeness of men so we could be made like Him. In Philippians 3:20,21 Paul wrote from his prison cell, "For our conversation [citizenship] is in heaven; from whence also we look for the Saviour, the Lord Jesus Christ: Who shall change our vile body, that it may be fashioned like unto his glorious body...." The same expression is found, '...made in the fashion of a man.' What is He going to do when He comes? He is going to "change our vile body, that it may be fashioned like unto his glorious body, according to the working whereby he is able even to subdue all things unto himself."

I'm going to be like Jesus. That is sweet to my heart because that is the longing of my heart. Don't you want to be like Him? Won't it be wonderful when He comes?

Paul wrote of it, "Behold, I shew you a mystery; We shall not all sleep, but we shall all be changed, In a moment, in the twinkling of an eye, at the last trump: for the trumpet shall sound, and the dead shall be raised incorruptible" (I Cor. 15:51,52). We are going to be changed and we are going to be like Jesus.

I had a sweet first cousin who died at the age of thirteen, little Bobby Hamilton. The reason we started singing in our church an old southern song, "The Land Where Living Waters Flow" was that it was a favorite of little Bobby Hamilton. On his sickbed, from which he never arose, he quoted the twenty-third Psalm and asked his mother to sing, "The Land Where Living Waters Flow."

I thought so much of little Bobby. And of our sweet little twenty-two-day-old baby. And of my brother's sweet little two-and-a-half-year-old girl which died on my mother's birthday. I thought of how death has come and our hearts have been broken and the loneliness, sorrow and tears. Then I thought, Oh, yes, someday we are going to see them and be like Him.

I remembered something about little Bobby. When he was a little boy, and I was in the home of my aunt, she bought him some new clothes. She told Bobby to go in the other room and put on his new clothes. Little Bobby had on his play clothes and had something in every pocket. I don't know what all: stones, marbles, slingshot, maybe a bull frog or two, I don't know—little country boy, little sweet, Christian boy, Bobby. When he went out of the bedroom his pockets were filled with these stones, marbles and all the things little boys carry in their pockets. He went in and put on his new clothes; when he came back his pockets were bulging the same way.

His mother said, "Bobby, take all that junk out of your pockets." He began to take it all out and smoothe down his pockets; he brushed down his clothes and stood straight and tall so his mother could see how he looked.

I've often thought, Oh, this linen robe is perfect in the eyes of God, but it sometimes looks awfully bumpy and lumpy and spotted to the outsider. 'But when the Lord comes we shall see Him as He is.' Oh, to be like Him! That is the heart-cry of every true believer.

He was made in the likeness of a man so that I might be made in the likeness of Christ.

'He was made in the likeness of men.'—Phil. 2:8.

THE BAPTISM OF JESUS CHRIST

"And Jesus, when he was baptized, went up straightway out of the water: and, lo, the heavens were opened unto him, and he saw the Spirit of God descending like a dove, and lighting upon him."—Matt. 3:16.

I. The Master's Baptism

II. The Mode of Baptism—Only One

III. The Meaning of Baptism

IV. The Misunderstanding of Baptism

V. The Misinterpretation of Scriptures on Baptism

The Jordan River

"Then cometh Jesus from Galilee to Jordan unto John, to be baptized of him."—Matt. 3:13.

3

The Baptism of Jesus Christ

"And Jesus, when he was baptized, went up straightway out of the water: and, lo, the heavens were opened unto him, and he saw the Spirit of God descending like a dove, and lighting upon him."—Matt. 3:16.

All four of the Gospels give the account of the baptism of Jesus Christ by His own cousin, John the Baptist, in the River Jordan. You ask what is so significant about that. I call to your memory the fact that all four of the Gospels do not give an account of the virgin birth of Jesus Christ. All four of the Gospels do not give an account of His glorious, miraculous ascension back into the presence of the Father after His work of redemption was finished on earth. All four of the Gospels do not give an account of all of His great miracles and His great sermons. But all four of the Gospels give record of the baptism of Jesus Christ by water in the River Jordan. This alone would give importance to it. This is a doctrinal subject.

All doctrine in the Bible points back to Jesus Christ. It is like the spokes in a wheel. Every spoke points away from the rim of the wheel back to the hub. So, every doctrine in the Bible points to Jesus Christ. The doctrine of believer's baptism points to the Lord Jesus Himself.

Notice another thing before we deal with the subject, and that is, the baptism of Jesus in the River Jordan was the beginning of His public ministry. Jesus was thirty years of age. No public ministry had begun until that glorious day when the blessed Master came walking down the banks of the Jordan and asked John to baptize Him just exactly like you and I were baptized after we were saved.

It was the baptism that began the ministry of Jesus and a baptism that ended His ministry. The baptism that began it was a baptism of water. The baptism that ended it was a baptism of fire and of judgment and death in the sinner's place.

You remember that there had been an argument among the disciples. It was brought about because two of them, James and John, had made their mother come with them to Jesus and make a request. The mother of James and John said to Jesus, "Grant that these my two sons may sit, the one on thy right hand, and the other on the left, in thy kingdom." The answer was: "Ye know not what ye ask. Are ye able to drink of the cup that I shall drink of, and to be baptized with the baptism that I am baptized with?" (Matt. 20:22). And He spoke of the awful sufferings of Gethsemane, of Pilate's judgment hall and of Calvary. So His ministry began with water baptism and ended in a fiery baptism of the outpouring of the judgment of God upon Him as He took your place and mine.

I want you to notice five truths in the Bible on the subject of "believer's baptism."

I. The Master's Baptism

First of all, notice the Master's baptism, the baptism of Jesus Christ Himself. The baptism of Jesus shows its extreme importance.

On any subject that relates to your peace of mind and your obedience to God and the happiness of your heart, the Devil would have you go too far one way or too far the other way. He would have you burn to death or freeze to death, but he never wants you to go down the middle of the road exactly like you ought to go. There are some who put too much importance on baptism and say that you cannot be saved without it. There are others who put too little emphasis on it and say the only thing of importance is that you be saved and that nothing else really matters.

The baptism of Jesus Christ teaches us its tremendous importance. Mark 1:9 says, "And it came to pass in those days, that Jesus came from Nazareth of Galilee, and was baptized of John in Jordan." Stop and think of this verse and its teaching. See the picture of it. Jesus came from Nazareth, in Galilee, to John to be baptized by him in the River Jordan. Stop and consider where John was baptizing. The Jordan runs a good many miles from the foot of Mount Hermon, the highest mountain in Palestine. Mount Hermon is more than nine thousand feet high, and every month of the year white snow from it melts and runs into the Sea of Galilee, then down the Jordan River, and empties into the Dead Sea some sixty or seventy miles away.

Now at what place in the Jordan was John baptizing? The Scriptures teach us that he was baptizing somewhere at Bethabara, probably also called Bethany, on the Jordan River some twenty-two miles east of Jerusalem. This means that Jesus Christ, if He came "as straight as the crow flies," walked sixty miles in order to be baptized.

Don't you ever tell me that baptism is not important! If the blessed Son of God walked all the way from Nazareth, in Galilee, down to the River Jordan even with Jerusalem in order to be baptized, the baptism of the Master teaches the importance of the baptism of the believer.

It teaches in the second place that baptism is not efficacious, or that baptism does not save. Why was Jesus baptized? In the third chapter of Matthew you find that John the Baptist, who was a cousin of the Lord Jesus and six months older than Jesus, was preaching. In verse 8 John says, "Bring forth therefore fruits meet for repentance." Now why did John say that?

Some people had come to be baptized who, John knew, had never repented of their sins and were not saved. John refused to baptize unsaved people, so he said to them, "You cannot be baptized until you bring forth fruits meet for repentance."

Now, what about Jesus Christ, the Son of God, who never sinned—the altogether lovely One; the absolutely holy One; the entirely perfect One? How is He to "bring forth fruits meet for repentance"? That is why when Jesus came to the River Jordan to be baptized, John was reluctant and said, "I have need to be baptized of thee." But Jesus said, 'No, go ahead and baptize Me; for thus it becometh us to fulfill all righteousness.'

Jesus was baptized and He never needed to repent; He never needed to be saved. He was the absolutely perfect One. And here we are shown that baptism doesn't save one, because here is One baptized who didn't need to be saved. So I learned from the baptism of Jesus that baptism is not efficacious, or that it does not save.

People often say to me, "You name one man in the Bible like you or me who was saved but wasn't baptized, and went to Heaven." These people tell me, "Unless you are baptized, you cannot enter Heaven, you cannot be saved."

I can name one. He died on a cross. He turned to Jesus in his dying hour and said, "Lord, remember me when thou comest into thy kingdom," and Jesus said to him who was never baptized; never observed the Lord's Supper; never, so far as I know, did one good thing for God, "To day shalt thou be with me in paradise" (Luke 23:43).

This Bible does not teach the subject of so-called baptismal regeneration, and the baptism of Jesus Christ proves that baptism is not efficacious.

In the third place, this baptism of Jesus shows that baptism pleases God. I wish I had the time to deal with some things about the baptism of Jesus that we sometimes overlook. The Bible says, for instance, that He was praying (Luke 3:21). After Jesus was baptized, the heavens opened and an audible Voice spoke (this Voice was the Father), and He said, "This is my beloved Son, in whom I am well pleased" (Matt. 3:17). Only two other times did God ever break the heavens and disturb the silence and speak that way of Jesus; one was in John 12:28 and the other was at the transfiguration. But when Jesus was baptized of John beneath the water of the River Jordan, God from Heaven said, "This is my beloved Son, in whom I am well pleased."

That teaches me that God is pleased when a person follows Jesus Christ immediately in believer's baptism. The whole Trinity was there. When Jesus was baptized, there was the Son in the water, and the Bible says that the Holy Spirit in the form of a dove, came upon Him, and God the Father from Heaven spoke audibly. We are to be baptized in the name of the Father, and of the Son, and of the Holy Ghost, because every member of the Trinity was tremendously represented at the baptism of Jesus Christ.

Then, in studying the baptism of Jesus as it is recorded in the four Gospels, I found that the baptism of Jesus was a thing that publicly identified Him to the people as the true Christ, the true Messiah. Let me show you what I mean. In the Gospel of John, chapter 1, is one record of the baptism of Jesus. These are the words that you read in John 1:32-34.

"And John bare record, saying, I saw the Spirit descending from heaven like a dove, and it abode upon him. And I knew him not: but he that sent me to baptize with water, the same said unto me, Upon whom thou shalt see the Spirit descending, and remaining on him, the same is he which baptizeth with the Holy Ghost. And I saw, and bare record that this is the Son of God."

God said to John, 'When One comes along to be baptized of you, and you see the Holy Spirit of God coming upon Him and remaining upon Him, then you nail it down, and mark it down that that is the One who is the Son of God.'

In the Old Testament in the story of Jacob's ladder you see angels coming and going, but here you see the Holy Spirit of God coming and remaining. God said to John, 'When you see that happen, you will know that this is the

Christ. He is the Messiah. He is My Son, the Saviour of the world.'

That day when John baptized Jesus in the Jordan, the Holy Spirit of God came upon the blessed Master. No wonder John cried out, "Behold the Lamb of God, which taketh away the sin of the world" (John 1:29). The Son has come, the Saviour of the world! It was authenticated by the baptism of Jesus in the River Jordan.

I want to mention something that I have pondered about ever since I have been a Christian. I have studied it carefully because there is a mystery here to which I must confess I do not have the answer. When John said to Jesus, "I have need to be baptized of thee, and comest thou to me?" he was saying, in substance, what Peter said: "I am a sinful man! O Lord, I am not worthy to baptize You!" Jesus said, "Suffer it to be so now: for thus it becometh us to fulfill all righteousness."

I am not going to be technical, but there are two kinds of righteousness in the Bible, an outward righteousness and an imputed righteousness. Let me show you what I mean by that.

I do not care who you are; when you are saved, when you become a Christian, you have imputed unto you the righteousness of Jesus Christ. Like the father who put a robe on the returning prodigal, God clothes every born-again Christian in the white linen of the spotless righteousness of Jesus Christ.

There is another kind of righteousness mentioned in I John 3:7, "...he that doeth righteousness is righteous, even as he is righteous." What Jesus is saying is, 'I want to do the righteous thing, and I want to do what any person ought to do.' This is an act of outward righteousness on the part of Jesus Christ.

I read that on the day of Pentecost, "They that gladly received his word were baptized.... And the Lord added to the church daily such as should be saved" (Acts 2:41,47). I say to you that when you are genuinely saved, properly taught, you won't have to be dragged into the pool. They that gladly received the Word of God were just as gladly baptized. Jesus said, "...thus it becometh us to fulfill all righteousness."

There is another meaning to it. Jesus is saying, 'This will identify Me as the Son of God. I came to accomplish the whole plan of the righteousness of God; to pay the debt of sin; to die upon the cross. This is the beginning of My public ministry. Thus it becometh us to fulfill all righteousness.'

Jesus here sets an example. I am so glad that the Lord was baptized by immersion in water, because if He hadn't been, you would talk about people getting saved and then baptized and you would hear again and again, "Well, Jesus wasn't baptized." I thank God that no one can ever say, Jesus wasn't baptized, but I can say, Jesus was baptized, and you need to be baptized when you are saved. He did it to be our perfect Example, "...leaving us an example, that ye should follow his steps" (I Pet. 2:21).

Let me give you this testimony. I was saved in a Methodist Episcopal Church South. A man, praying, said, "Lord, bless the Methodist Church." Someone listening to the man praying said, "That is the Methodist Episcopal Church South he is talking about, Lord; that is the one he wants blessed." Well, that is the one I was saved in. They used to have great revivals, but now there is one big church of great confusion. I got out of one bunch that went modern and got into the Methodist Protestant, and finally they went together; so I got out of the whole thing.

But I was saved in a Methodist church. The old-fashioned circuit-riding preacher used to tell us in an old country church, "I will baptize you by the mode of your choice." I had just been saved as a country boy. Three days before I was saved a contest was going on between the young people, with credit being given for reading so many chapters of the

Bible, attending all the services, bringing other people, etc. So in three days' time I read every word of the New Testament. As an unsaved, uneducated, untrained country boy, I got the impression the Bible taught that the proper mode of baptism was by immersion; so I said to the preacher, "I want you to baptize me by immersion." And a group of us went to the creek and were baptized in it by a Methodist preacher. I answered the call to preach and went away to Bob Jones College. I got to thinking about baptism, believer's baptism, and who had the right to baptize, when to be baptized, what baptism means; and the thought came to me: Could anything be wrong with my baptism? I was baptized in a church that said: We will sprinkle you or baptize you by immersion in water. I had been baptized the right way, but I had questions in my mind. I prayed about it for awhile; then I met an ordained Baptist preacher who was pastor of a little Baptist church down in Lafayette, Georgia. One night I went to that ordained Baptist preacher and said to him, "I have been saved and baptized by immersion, but I still have some questions about my baptism. I can't sleep well at night, I think of it so often; and I want to be absolutely right. I am going into the ministry. I don't ever want the Devil to say to me that there is something wrong with my salvation, something wrong with my baptism, something wrong with my call to the ministry." I said to the preacher, "If you will, I want you to baptize me."

So one morning before daylight, the preacher and I, with the Scriptures in our hands, quoted from the Bible and fellowshiped together as we walked a mile from the dormitory to a little lake. We waded out into that lake. It was autumn, and brown leaves had fallen from the trees onto the water. About the time the sun came up, we raked the leaves back out of the way and lifted our voices to God and prayed. The preacher lifted up his hand and said, "I baptize thee, my brother, Tom Malone, in the name of the Father, and of the Son, and of the Holy Ghost." He placed me down beneath the surface of the water and brought me up again. We put our arms around each other and wept and praised the Lord, and went back together. From that hour until this I have never doubted that I have completely obeyed the Son of God as a believer by being scripturally baptized.

Have you been saved and baptized as the Bible teaches?

"And Jesus, when he was baptized, went up straightway out of the water: and, lo, the heavens were opened unto him, and he saw the Spirit of God descending like a dove, and lighting upon him: And lo a voice from heaven, saying, This is my beloved Son, in whom I am well pleased."— Matt. 3:16,17.

II. The Mode of Baptism—Only One

Following the subject of the Master's baptism, I want you to notice secondly the mode of baptism. There has been only one mode of baptism in all the history of the church since the beginning of the writing of the New Testament books of the blessed Bible. Never have there been two. When anyone asks what mode of baptism you follow, practice, or believe in, you could correctly answer, "There is only one mode of baptism." The Bible teaches only one mode.

We have today the King James Version of the Bible. It was only a few generations ago that King James I of England asked some fifty or more scholars to translate the Scriptures into a version which would be called after him, King James. That is why we have this version. The word for baptism in the New Testament comes from a Greek word *baptizo*, a form of the Greek word *bapto*. When they came to the word for "baptism," these scholars came back to the King and said, "When we translate this as it ought to be translated, it is going to cause trouble in the Church of England, the Anglican Church. The Anglican Church sprinkles, but we translate this word for baptism as it is found in the New Testament. There is only one way to translate it. It must be translated: 'to immerse,' 'to dip under,' 'to submerge,' and the mode of baptism is by immersion in water." The King said, "Instead of translating it, let's transliterate it, that is, let's coin a word for *bapto*—'to immerse,' 'to dip under,' 'to submerge.'" Thus in the King James Version of the Bible there is a transliteration, an English spelling, not a translation, of the word. The translation would not be "baptism," but "immersion," "submersion," or "dipping under." A word coined in the King James Version is the word "baptism." There is no teaching in the Scripture at all on the mode of baptism except that it is to be by immersion, submersion, or dipping under—by immersion in water.

Some people will say there is another word for baptism. In the Greek New Testament the word *rhantizo* is the word translated "sprinkling." Never one time in all the Scriptures is the word "sprinkling" used in connection with baptism of a believer after he has been saved. There is never an instance in the Bible where anyone was ever sprinkled in all the history of the Word of God, that is, sprinkled as a mode of baptism.

It was at least 150 or 200 years after Pentecost before any church, anywhere, at any time, ever thought of such a thing as practicing sprinkling as a so-called mode of baptism. Then the circumstance arose where people who were saved could not come to the baptismal pool. The church leaders said, "What can we do? They cannot come to be baptized. We will take baptism to them." There is never an instance in the Scripture where baptism was ever taken to anyone. But about 150 or 200 years after Pentecost they said, "People are sick. They cannot come. What shall we do?" Then churches departed from the Scripture and changed the whole meaning of baptism, before they ever changed the mode of baptism, and they took baptism to the candidate and sprinkled him. But by biblical interpretation no one ever gets any mode of baptism except by immersion in water. I will give you some Scriptures for this.

Matthew 3:5,6 reads: "Then went out to him [John] Jerusalem, and all Judaea, and all the region round about Jordan, And were baptized of him in Jordan, confessing their sins." It does not say *at* the Jordan but *IN* the Jordan.

Let me read you some other Scriptures to see if there is any room whatsoever for any mode of baptism except by immersion in water. In John 3:23 we read: "And John also was baptizing in Aenon near to Salim, because there was much water there: and they came, and were baptized." Here you read John baptized in a certain place "because there was much water there," and the people came where much water was in order to be baptized.

In Matthew 3:16 we read of the baptism of the Lord Jesus Christ. "And Jesus, when he was baptized, went up straightway out of the water...." No one could ever get "sprinkling" from that.

There are many occasions of water baptism in Acts. In the eighth chapter of Acts is recorded the baptism of the Ethiopian eunuch. When Deacon Philip caught a ride with him across the desert, the eunuch was saved. There are three verses of Scripture in the eighth chapter of Acts — verses 36, 38, and 39, in which there are three statements that I want you to notice. First of all, we read that when they came to a place where there was "certain water," the Ethiopian eunuch, who had just believed in Jesus Christ as his personal Saviour, said, "See, here is water...."

Now, just think for a moment. Do you think that Ethiopian eunuch, or Philip, going down across the desert, down toward Gaza, didn't have drinking water with them? Do you think they didn't have any water with them when they came to a place where there was "certain water"? But they didn't have enough water for him to be baptized in. It is not true, as the fellow said: "I could take a teacup of water and baptize everyone in the State of Ohio." I have taken the eighth chapter of the book of Acts and tried to read it and see if that would fit in there. Again I will try this. In verses 36-39 we read:

"And as they went on their way, they came unto a certain [teacupful of] *water: and the eunuch said, See, here is* [a teacupful of] *water; what doth hinder me to be baptized? And Philip said, If thou believest with all thine heart, thou mayest. And he answered and said, I believe that Jesus Christ is the Son of God. And he commanded the chariot to stand still: and they went down both into the* [teacupful of] *water, both Philip and the eunuch; and he baptized him. And when they were come up out of the* [teacupful of] *water, the Spirit of the Lord caught away Philip...."*

It just doesn't work, does it? It doesn't fit there! "... they went down *both* into the water, *both* Philip and the eunuch.... And when *they were come up out of the water*, the Spirit of the Lord caught away Philip...."

So in every single instance where water baptism is taught in the Bible, there is but one mode of baptism, and that is by immersion. I know this in other ways which I cannot dwell on now. I know by biblical archeology. The ruins of early churches all had pools, such as the pools at Jerusalem, the pool at the ruins of Corinth, and other places where there were New Testament churches. Archeologists have found pools where people were baptized. So the mode of baptism is only one; there never has been but one; never could be but one, if it is to be scriptural; and that mode is by immersion in water.

"And Jesus, when he was baptized, went up straightway out of the water: and, lo, the heavens were opened unto him, and he saw the Spirit of God descending like a dove, and lighting upon him: And lo a voice from heaven, saying, This is my beloved Son, in whom I am well pleased."—Matt. 3:16, 17.

III. The Meaning of Baptism

I come to the third thing and that is the meaning of baptism. What does it mean for a person to be baptized in water by immersion?

First, it is a picture of the Gospel of our Lord and Saviour Jesus Christ. Every time you see a person baptized, you see a visible picture of our Lord Jesus Christ and His Gospel. The Gospel is defined in I Corinthians 15:3,4. Paul said, "I delivered unto you first of all that which I also received, how that Christ died for our sins according to the scriptures; And that he was buried, and that he rose again the third day according to the scriptures."

You ask me, "What is the Gospel?" Many folks may not agree, but here is the definition of the Gospel. There are three things: the death, the burial, and resurrection of Jesus Christ. The Second Coming is not a part of the Gospel. The ascension is not a part of the Gospel; it is a part of the Word of God, an essential part, a wonderful part. But when Paul defined the Gospel he said there were three things: the death on the cross, the burial in the tomb, and the resurrection of Jesus Christ, all according to the Scripture. That is the Gospel, Paul said, when he defines it in the Word of God.

When you see a believer baptized, you see an outward demonstration of all this Bible teaches that the Gospel is. You see one buried in the likeness of His death and raised in the likeness of His resurrection to walk in newness of life. So every time a person is baptized here, we are saying, This church, this preacher baptizing, this candidate being baptized, believes the Gospel as it is set forth in the Word of God: "That Christ died for our sins according to the scriptures; And that he was buried, and that he rose again the third day according to the scriptures." So baptism is the picture of the Gospel of our Lord Jesus Christ.

In the second place, baptism is a picture of conversion. Now some Bible students say Romans 6 is the greatest passage of Scripture in the Bible on the subject of believer's baptism. I don't know if that is true or not, but I do know it is a great passage on the subject. In Romans 6 we see that believer's baptism pictures not only the Gospel but pictures conversion also. Verses 3-5 read:

"Know ye not, that so many of us as were baptized into Jesus Christ were baptized into his death? Therefore we are buried with him by baptism into death: that like as Christ was raised up from the dead by the glory of the Father, even so we also should walk in newness of life. For if we have been planted together in the likeness of his death, we shall be also in the likeness of his resurrection."

Notice two words here. First Paul said, "...we are buried...." People are not buried on top of the ground. Secondly he said, "...we have been planted...." You do not plant things on top of the ground. Two words here prove beyond any doubt that baptism is by immersion. We have been "buried"; we have been "planted." It is a picture of what is taking place inside a person.

When a candidate for baptism walks into the pool, he is saying, "I have died to the old life; I have a new life in Christ; and I am going to walk in that new life." When he is placed under the water, it is a picture that all his sins have been blotted out, as with a thick cloud, and removed as far as the East is from the West, put behind the back of God forever and remembered no more. The sin question with its penalty has all been settled and is past for that person. When he comes up out of the water, he is coming up saying, "I have a new life now, thank God, a resurrection life, a life kept by Jesus at the throne; and in that life I propose to walk." So baptism is a picture of conversion.

Baptism in the third place is a public confession of faith in Jesus Christ. Now I know that this confession can be made in other ways, but I believe with all my heart that the proof of conversion followed by baptism is important. As I said earlier in my message, there are those who say baptism is not important at all. That is why I take it as my subject. When I know that Jesus walked sixty or seventy miles, waded out into the muddy Jordan, and insisted that His cousin, John the Baptist, baptize Him, no one will ever make me think it is not important. There are others who say it is all-important, that no one can be saved without being baptized. But I am saying to you that in New Testament days, a testimony of conversion—not in order to be saved, but a positive, outward evidence that a person had been saved—was his baptism by immersion in water.

Now you read in Acts 2:41, "Then they that gladly received his word were baptized: and the same day there were added [this is where you get your additions to the church] unto them about three thousand souls." So they that gladly received His word were baptized, and baptism is a public confession of faith in Jesus Christ.

Now let's read an instance of that. Acts 22:16 is a verse that is misused many times. There are three chapters in the book of Acts that deal with the conversion of the Apostle Paul. In chapter 9 there is the historical and inspired record written by Luke (the Holy Spirit through Luke) telling how Paul was saved. Two other times in the book of Acts, Paul himself told how he was saved. Once to the Jews and once to the Gentiles he gives his testimony.

In Acts 22, when he is giving his testimony about how he was saved, he mentions something that is not even mentioned in Acts 9, where the actual account of his conversion is given. That is something Ananias said to him. You know, when Paul was saved, the Lord struck him blind. God made an example of him. That is something Paul wrote to Timothy, that he was an example, "a pattern." And God made a real example of him. He walked arrogantly on his way to Damascus, going to arrest more Christians and have them put to death. He had stood by the day Stephen was stoned, so God was going to deal with Paul in an unusual way. A light which blinded him shone from Heaven, and it was there on the Damascus road that Paul asked two questions: "Who art thou, Lord?" and "Lord, what wilt thou have me to do?" The Lord said to him, "Arise, and go into the city, and it shall be told thee what thou must do."

The Lord then spoke to Ananias and said, "I want you to go talk to Saul of Tarsus."

Ananias said, "I am afraid of him; he has killed Christians."

God said, "He prays now; you do not need to be afraid of him." So Ananias went and dealt with Paul.

Chapter 9 does not give it, but when Paul tells it years later to the Jews, he said that Ananias said to him these words: "And now why tarriest thou? arise, and be baptized, and wash away thy sins, calling on the name of the Lord" (Acts 22:16). What did Ananias say? He did not say, "Arise and be baptized in order to be saved." He said, "Paul, three days ago Jesus Christ spoke to you, three days ago you repented, three days ago you were smitten down, three days ago God dealt with you, three days ago you saw Jesus, recognized Him, yielded to Him, submitted to Him; now be baptized and let people know your sins have been forgiven."

I say to you now, baptism by immersion in water is one real, honest, biblical way a person can witness that he has been saved. If anyone hears this truth from the Word of God, he ought to obey it. I am even going to go further and say that I have some doubts and misgivings about people who make a public profession of faith and being taught the command of Christ, do not follow the Lord in believer's baptism, because the Bible says that when people got saved, they got baptized. That was the only way they could show they had a right to be called "Christian," and it was a public confession of their faith.

"And Jesus, when he was baptized, went up straightway out of the water: and, lo, the heavens were opened unto him, and he saw the Spirit of God descending like a dove, and lighting upon him: And lo a voice from heaven, saying, This is my beloved Son, in whom I am well pleased."—Matt. 3:16, 17.

IV. The Misunderstanding of Baptism

In the fourth place I want you to see the misunderstanding of baptism. I am listing five things not taught in the Bible, five misunderstandings about baptism that people have developed through the years.

There is, for one thing, the matter of infant baptism. People say, "We baptize babies at our church." We don't in the Emmanuel Baptist Church. We dedicate them, but we do not baptize them. There is not one Scripture in the Bible that would teach infant baptism. People say, "Well, you read in the sixteenth chapter of Acts about the household of Lydia and the household of the Philippian jailer. It says all their household, all their family, were baptized at once." So what? That doesn't mean anything. You read, for instance, of the Philippian jailer "believing with all his house," every one of them old enough to believe, and people say, "All of his house, the whole family, were baptized. Some of them must have been babies." That is poor reasoning and not Bible. Every one of them were old enough to believe. Acts 16:34 teaches this.

Lydia (her husband was not even mentioned) is already down by the riverside. She is already in a prayer meeting when she hears the Gospel, and she and her household were baptized. There is not an instance in the Bible of infant baptism.

Someone handed me a tract which said, "Herein is contained all the Scriptures that deal with infant baptism." I opened up the tract and on the inside were two clean pages. I said, "Amen! Hallelujah! Praise the Lord!"

That's all there is to it. There isn't anything in the Bible about infant baptism, not one single word. Many a person tonight is on his way to Hell, lost without God and without hope, depending on the fact that some misguided parent took him in his arms when he was just a little baby, had a few drops of water sprinkled into his face and he is claiming that as his hope of Heaven, and there is no hope.

When Mrs. Malone and I lived on Rundell Street in Pontiac, a lady came to our home one day. (At that time I was on the radio every morning and I had people writing and calling me about a good many things.) This lady came with a little baby in her arms and a more elderly lady was with her, who was her mother and the grandmother of the little baby. I invited them into the living room. There stood these two people, the grandmother, her daughter, and her little baby girl in her arms.

The mother said, "We drove all the way from Capac, Michigan. We drove fifty miles or so down here because we hear you every morning on the radio and I want you to baptize my little girl."

I wanted to be tactful and kind; I did not want to be offensive, but I said, "I could not possibly baptize your little baby girl."

The woman said, "Well, I am disappointed. We came a long way and wanted you to do it. We have listened to you on the radio. We have heard you preach the Word of God. We have enjoyed it so much and wanted you to be the one to baptize our little baby girl."

I began to try to show her the Scriptures. I told her that the Scriptures do not teach infant baptism. I asked her, "Is there any Scripture you can think of that teaches it?" She had some that she mentioned that I have already mentioned to you which have no reference whatsoever to infant baptism.

In a moment I looked at her, the mother of that little eighteen-month-old baby, and said, "Lady, could I ask you a question? Are you a Christian? Are you saved? Do you know today as you sit in this room, that you have been born the second time and that you are on your way to Heaven?"

She said, "I sure do."

I said, "That's fine. That's wonderful. I am glad of that. Now, I would like to ask you another question. What makes you believe that you have been born again, that you are saved, that your sins are forgiven and that you are on your way to Heaven today?"

She said, "Because my mother (and she pointed to that gray-haired grandmother) took me when I was this baby's age and had me baptized in the church. That is why I know I am a Christian and I know my sins are forgiven and I know I am on my way to Heaven."

And I said, "My dear lady, you do not have one word of Scripture, not one syllable of Scripture, to give you any hope of ever getting to Heaven if you are depending on infant baptism. It is not taught in the Bible. I am doing you a great favor by not baptizing her, because you are lost, depending for yourself on what you want me to do for her. Then she would be lost."

I found out the grandmother was lost, too. Neither one of them knew anything about the Lord.

You say to me, "Why preach so much on baptism?" Because of the false teachings. There are souls this moment who are being damned and are on their way to Hell, because of a misunderstanding of this Bible teaching.

There is another misunderstanding of baptism. Some people have been baptized before they were converted and so they are not scripturally baptized. In the Bible, baptism is always subsequent to conversion. In every single instance —not a single exception—baptism always follows conversion.

I quote again the Ethiopian eunuch who after he had been reading Isaiah 53 and Philip had begun preaching about Jesus, said, "See, here is water; what doth hinder me to be baptized?" And Philip said, "If thou believest with all thine heart, thou mayest." And he, the Ethiopian eunuch, answered and said, "I believe that Jesus Christ is the Son of God." He said, "I believe." Then Philip said, "We will stop this chariot right here," and Philip baptized him after he was saved. No one anywhere in the Bible ever was scripturally baptized before conversion.

There is a third erroneous teaching I wish I had more time to deal with. It is a sermon in itself. That is what people call "baptismal regeneration." Preachers for years have written me trying to get me to publicly debate on the subject of baptism. I am not going to. If people want to hear me debate, they can hear me three times on Sunday and on Wednesday night in the Emmanuel Baptist Church of Pontiac. I debate all the time! These preachers write letters and want me to debate on baptism and they say that the Bible teaches baptismal regeneration, that is, you are saved by being baptized.

If I had the time, I would like to lay a foundation of what this Bible teaches about being saved. John 1:11 and 12 says, "He came unto his own, and his own received him not. But as many as received him, to them gave he power [authority] to become the sons of God, even to them that believe on his name." Not one word said about being baptized.

In Acts 16:30 the Philippian jailer asked, "What must I do to be saved? And they said, Believe on the Lord Jesus Christ, and thou shalt be saved, and thy house." Not one word about being baptized as yet.

Romans 5:1 says, "Therefore being justified by faith, we have peace with God through our Lord Jesus Christ." Justification, and not one word about being baptized.

Galatians 3:26 says, "For ye are all the children of God by faith in Christ Jesus." Not one word said about being baptized in that verse.

Titus 3:5 says, "Not by works of righteousness which we have done, but according to his mercy he saved us, by the washing of regeneration, and renewing of the Holy Ghost."

Let me say this, Jesus said that the new birth was from above, didn't He? Baptism is something you do on earth. Conversion is something God performs and it comes from above. No human work has anything in the world to do with salvation through faith, by grace, and from God Himself. So baptismal regeneration is not taught in the Bible.

Let us take Jesus by Himself. You read in John, chapter 4, a statement that says, "Though Jesus himself baptized not, but his disciples" (vs. 2). Jesus did not baptize, but His disciples. Don't you think if baptism were required to be saved, that Jesus Christ would have been a baptizer? But the Bible says, "Though Jesus himself baptized not, but his disciples." You will never make me believe that anyone who loved sinners as much as Jesus, the Son of God, did, wouldn't have been trying to get people baptized as fast as He could get them to repent, if it were a requisite for salvation.

When Paul was writing to the people of Corinth in chapter 1 of I Corinthians, in verse 14 he said, "I thank God that I baptized none of you, but Crispus and Gaius." Then he thought further and said, "And I baptized also the household of Stephanas: besides, I know not whether I baptized any other."

You want to tell me that salvation depends on being baptized, yet Jesus Christ never baptized and Paul never baptized but three families in all of their ministry. There is no such thing taught in the Bible as baptismal regeneration.

Then there is another misunderstanding about baptism. That is a "probationary period." We have a short one in the Emmanuel Baptist Church and even that is too long. If you get saved in the Emmanuel Baptist Church in the morning, you probably would not get baptized until the evening service, and that is too long a wait. If we could get away from that and do it just exactly like they did in the Bible, God would bless us for it. But this business of probation...I know great missionary societies say, "On the foreign field it is different." Listen, baptism started on a foreign field. Anyone ought to know that. It didn't start in Pontiac. It started on the foreign field. Then these missionaries would come around and say, "On the foreign field we put them on

probation for twelve months." Now that sounds good and it
sounds pious, but I was preaching along this line one time
and a missionary was right here and said to me, "You
couldn't do that on a foreign field."

I said, "Listen, I believe that the same Bible and the same
teaching and the same methods work in the darkest part of
Africa just like God wants them to work in the city of Pontiac, Michigan."

There is no probationary period set forth in the Bible.

I have mentioned the Ethiopian eunuch who said, "What
doth hinder me to be baptized." Philip said, "Nothing.
Right now if you are a Christian, stop this chariot, get down
and get in the pool." (A few months ago I stood at the place
between Jerusalem and Hebron where it is said that Philip
baptized the Ethiopian eunuch.)

I love the 16th chapter of Acts. I get in it and go wild! I
am like a little boy in a toy shop. I get in this chapter of
Acts and I find some things and I turn cartwheels inside. It
is such a wonderful chapter. I love to read of the conversion of the Philippian jailer. He was about to take his life;
Paul said, "Do thyself no harm." He fell down and cried,
"What must I do to be saved?" Paul and Silas said, "Believe
on the Lord Jesus Christ, and thou shalt be saved, and thy
house." The Bible says that he believed with all of his
household and that night was saved.

Now I want to mention something. You talk about a probationary period. The earthquake didn't come until midnight. Some time between midnight and dawn the jailer and
all of his family got baptized. Now, the average Baptist
preacher would have said, "We will take care of it next
Sunday night." Or at the very best he would have said,
"The next time we have a church service you will be baptized."

Many preachers in the South will say, "You have to have
a proper mode, proper candidate, and proper authority."
They say, "If anyone were to be baptized by an individual

out in the lake somewhere, he would not be scripturally baptized because it is not by church authority."

Listen, Jesus said, "Where two or three are gathered together in my name, there am I in the midst of them." I want to show you something.

How many people were there present when Philip baptized the Ethiopian eunuch? How many deacons were there? How many? One. One, that is all. How many preachers were there? One. The deacon and the preacher were the same one. How many voted for them to be baptized? Not a one! Many people preach something because the preacher before them preached it. But it is not in the Bible.

Here were two preachers in Acts 16, and not a deacon anywhere near in the world. I thank God for deacons, but that night there was not a deacon to be found. Here were two preachers, and they were beat half to death. The jailer got saved and the earthquake didn't come until after midnight. You read that that same hour of the night he washed their stripes and they were baptized, "he and all his, straightway." I would like to have seen that. I really would. I would like to have been a neighbor somewhere peeping out and looking over next door.

I can just see some old woman looking under the shade and saying, "There are some strange things going on over there tonight. Why, they have been up all night. It is two o'clock in the morning. The candles have been lit. It is almost morning and they have not gone to bed yet." The old man would say, "Move over, let me watch too." After a while he would say, "Why, they have all gone crazy. They have got on wash clothes and are leaving the house at two o'clock in the morning! I wonder where they are going." The old man probably would have said, "Why, I am going to follow them." Now this is not recorded in the Bible, so don't look for it. He said, "I am going to see." And he goes down by the riverside. Perhaps between one and two o'clock in the morning they were baptized. No probationary period. It is not taught in the Bible.

There is another misunderstanding I do not have the time to deal with. The Corinthians had gotten away from God and when he wrote in I Corinthians 15:29 he talked to them about being baptized "for the dead." When someone died that they hoped was a Christian, someone would say, "I am going to be baptized for him." Baptism by proxy is not taught in the Bible. It was an erroneous thing that the Corinthians did, and they did about everything wrong.

"And Jesus, when he was baptized, went up straightway out of the water: and, lo, the heavens were opened unto him . . . ."

V. The Misinterpretation of Scriptures on Baptism

The fifth thing I want to deal with is the misinterpretation of the baptism in the Scripture. I want to deal with three or four Scriptures that seem to teach that you have to be baptized in order to be saved.

First of all, in Mark 16:16 you read where Jesus said, "He that believeth and is baptized shall be saved; but he that believeth not shall be damned." Many people say, "Well, there Jesus plainly said, 'He that believeth and is baptized shall be saved.'" Now you interpret the Scriptures in the light of other Scriptures. You cannot isolate a passage and lift it out here and interpret it without the light of the other Scriptures shining on it. Jesus did not mean to teach here that you had to be baptized in order to be saved. For in the same verse He taught there is only one thing that condemns and that is unbelief. "He that believeth and is baptized shall be saved; but he that believeth not shall be damned."

Suppose that I would say to Mrs. Malone, "If you get on the train here in Pontiac and sit down (which is the customary thing to do), the train would take you to Detroit, Michigan." So I would say, "She that getteth on the train and sitteth down will go to Detroit."

Suppose the next day I would say, "Did you go to Detroit?"
"Yes, I did."
"Did you go on the train?"
"Yes, I went on the train."
"Did you find a seat?"
"No, they were all taken."
"You mean you stood up all the way?"
"Yes."

"Well, I said to you, 'She who getteth on the train and sitteth down will go to Detroit.' Now I find out that you went to Detroit and didn't sit down at all." But she went just the same. She went the same way everyone else did. Getting on the train is important; sitting down is not the main thing.

"He that believeth and is baptized shall be saved...." The important thing is the believing and not the baptizing. You are just as sure to be saved when you believe as you are sure you will get there when you get on a train to go to Detroit. You can stand up, sit down, hang out the window; you are going. When you believe, you are on your way, thank God. Doesn't that seem logical?

In John 3:5, Jesus answered, "Verily, verily, I say unto thee, Except a man be born of water and of the Spirit, he cannot enter into the kingdom of God." Someone says, "There you are; explain that one." I don't think it is difficult at all. In the first place, water in the Bible is typical of the Holy Spirit and of the Word of God. Many, many times it is used as a symbol of the Word and of the Holy Spirit. But there is a word in John 3:5, the word *kai* where it says, "Except a man be born of water *AND...*" as it is translated here, but it can be translated "even" and is translated "even" many times in the Scriptures. So this verse could just as easily be translated, "Except a man be born of water *EVEN* of the Spirit, he cannot enter into the kingdom of God." It is talking about the Holy Spirit of God.

There are other passages such as Acts 2:38 and I Peter

3:19-22. But isn't it wonderful, my friends, that salvation is by grace, unmerited favor, something you don't deserve! Jesus purchased it with His own blood on the cross. Isn't it worthwhile after you are saved, to look back to a finished work and say, "I will do anything God wants me to do now that I am saved"? The first thing that God wants a believer to do is to be baptized, just exactly like Jesus was—by immersion in water.

Let us look at these other two passages which seem to teach baptismal regeneration but do not.

As Peter preached on the day of Pentecost, great conviction fell on the people and they asked a great question, "Men and brethren, what shall we do?" (Acts 2:37). Now here is the answer: "Repent, and be baptized every one of you in the name of Jesus Christ for the remission of sins, and ye shall receive the gift of the Holy Ghost" (Acts 2:38). Now the key word here is *for* — "for the remission of sins." The Greek word is *eis* which can be translated *"because of"* or *"on account of."* We firmly believe that this passage teaches we are to be baptized because our sins have been forgiven, not in order that they might be remitted because of baptism.

Another passage often used, and just as often misused, is I Peter 3:20-22, "...while the ark was a preparing, wherein few, that is, eight souls were saved by water." Weymouth translates this verse, "A few persons eight in number were brought safely through the water." They were not saved "by" the water but "through" the water. The ark was a type of Christ and the means of safety and the waters were God's means of judgment. They were saved in spite of the water and not because of the water.

But someone says, "What about verse 21?" Notice this verse: "The like figure whereunto even baptism doth also now save us (not the putting away of the filth of the flesh, but the answer of a good conscience toward God,) by the resurrection of Jesus Christ."

Now the verse plainly says here that baptism is a "figure." It also says that baptism does not put away the filthiness of the flesh.

In the light of the Scriptures, these verses could not possibly teach baptismal regeneration. "Knowing this first, that no prophecy of the scripture is of any private interpretation" (II Pet. 1:20).

The Gospel of John tells us nearly one hundred times that we are saved by believing.

"For by grace are ye saved through faith; and that not of yourselves: it is the gift of God."—Eph. 2:8.

THE TRANSFIGURATION OF JESUS CHRIST

(Read: Matthew 16:28-17:13)

I. I See Here a Miraculous and Beautiful Prophetical Ful-fillment

II. I See in the Transfiguration of Jesus the Wonderful Power of Prayer

III. I Feel a Personal Love Demonstrated

IV. I See a Picture of Christ's Return

V. The Preeminence of Jesus

VI. I See Peter's Forgetting the Lost Multitude

VII. They Talked of His Death

Snowcapped Mount Hermon

View from a hillside near Tiberias, Israel, looking across the Sea of Galilee

4

The Transfiguration of Jesus Christ

I want to speak to you on one of those great themes in the Bible. It is one of the great, truly miraculous events in the earthly ministry and life of our Lord Jesus Christ. I am referring to the transfiguration of Jesus Christ.

I think we shall begin reading with Matthew 16:28, and read into chapter 17. Many Bible scholars and students say that verse 28 really should have been the first verse of chapter 17. In fact, in Mark 9 and Luke 9 there is no separation between these two verses, and actually in the other Gospels it begins the chapter on the transfiguration.

I have never preached on the transfiguration of Jesus, and I have been reading about it in the past few days and thinking about this glorious, wonderful thing that took place in the earthly ministry of Jesus, and of all the emphasis given to it in the first three books of the New Testament. Surely there is great significance to it, and surely the Lord has lessons for us to learn from the transfiguration of Jesus Christ.

It is interesting that five times in the book of Matthew we find Jesus undergoing a great mountaintop experience. In fact, there are five mountains mentioned in the book of Matthew where you find Jesus.

One is in chapter 5 where you find Him speaking on the Mount, that sermon we call the Sermon on the Mount. It was called that because Jesus went upon a mountain when He called the multitudes to Him and spake unto them that great sermon.

You find again in this great chapter here the transfiguration on the Mount.

In chapter 24 of Matthew, the longest discourse on the subject of prophecy Jesus gave sitting on the Mount of Olives, east of Jerusalem.

Chapter 27 of Matthew mentions the most wonderful, the most historical, the most sacred little mountain the world has ever known anything about, or ever will know—the hill called Mount Calvary. There Jesus was crucified.

In chapter 28 of Matthew and verse 16, we find Jesus after the resurrection on a mountain meeting with and commissioning His disciples.

As we come today to this Mount of Transfiguration and see Jesus glorified, let us see if we can get from the Word of God some truths that I believe the Lord would have us to know.

Mrs. Malone and I had the wonderful privilege of visiting the Vatican, the headquarters for all the Roman Catholic churches of the world. The Vatican is not just a group of buildings; the Vatican is a little country of about 110 acres, with its own post office, own government, own guards, own policemen, and several buildings, and the largest Catholic church (or basilica) in the world, St. Peter's. In that cathedral, over 600 feet long, owned by the Catholic Church, are some of the richest pieces of art to be found anywhere.

One is a picture painted by Raphael of the Transfiguration, a picture of Jesus with His face shining as bright as the flaming sun. You see two men in glorified bodies that have just come from Heaven. You see three awe-stricken disciples on that mountaintop as Jesus was transformed.

Today I would like for us to see not an artist's conception, but to see, if we can, a Bible picture of the transfiguration of Jesus Christ.

I find in reading and meditating upon these Scriptures seven glorious truths about the transfiguration, and I have listed all of these beginning with a capital P, if you would like to make a note of them and remember them.

"And was transfigured before them...."—Matt. 17:2.

I See Here a Miraculous and Beautiful Prophetical Fulfillment

Now, will you notice verse 28 of chapter 16. Jesus in chapter 16 has been talking to His disciples about His death. When He finished talking about His death, the crucifixion, the resurrection, and the suffering for the cause of God, in verse 28 He said, "Verily I say unto you, There be some standing here, which shall not taste of death, till they see the Son of man coming in his kingdom."

Now watch that closely. Jesus said to these disciples, "Some of you standing right in this group are never going to die until you see the Son of man coming in His kingdom." Now what did Jesus mean by that? Did He mean that before all these twelve men died, He was going to come again? Jesus makes a prophecy here that would seem unbelievable. He said, "There are some standing in this crowd that shall not taste of death until they have seen the Son of man coming in His kingdom."

Now every word of God must come to pass. If Jesus said, "Some of you are going to see Me come in My kingdom before you taste of death," then that Scripture must be fulfilled. Six days later the Scripture was fulfilled. Some believe that all these six days were spent walking from where they were at that time to the only snow-capped mountain in all that part of the country, Mount Hermon. Six days, some believe, they spent walking, and six days they spent, from where those words were spoken, getting up on top of that mountain. When they were up on top of that mountain, the words of Jesus were literally fulfilled. He said, "There are some of you who are not going to die until you see the Son of man coming in His kingdom and His power and His glory."

On that Mount of Transfiguration they saw a picture of His coming and a picture of His heavenly glory. Those dis-

ciples were taught once again that whatever Jesus says will
come to pass exactly as He says it will. Listen; some of
them got the lesson.

Years later Simon Peter wrote, "The word of the Lord
endureth for ever" (I Pet. 1:25). Simon Peter got convinced
that day that whatever Jesus predicts is going to happen,
will be fulfilled as He said it would. Peter said again concerning the second coming and the Bible:

*"For we have not followed cunningly devised fables, when
we made known unto you the power and coming of our Lord
Jesus Christ, but were eyewitnesses of his majesty. For he
received from God the Father honour and glory, when there
came such a voice to him from the excellent glory, This is
my beloved Son, in whom I am well pleased. And this voice
which came from heaven we heard, when we were with him
in the holy mount. We have also a more sure word of
prophecy; whereunto ye do well that ye take heed, as unto a
light that shineth in a dark place, until the day dawn, and
the day star arise in your hearts: Knowing this first, that
no prophecy of the scripture is of any private interpretation.
For the prophecy came not in old time by the will of man:
but holy men of God spake as they were moved by the Holy
Ghost."—II Pet. 1:16-21.*

That verse is the heart of the teaching of the Scriptures
on inspiration. When I opened the American Standard
Version to that verse, it didn't read, "All Scripture is giv-
en..." but, "Every scripture inspired of God is also profitable...." In other words, just pick out what you want that
you think *is given*. If you do not want to believe the book of
Jonah, don't believe it. If you do not want to believe the
story of creation in the book of Genesis, don't believe it!
Every scripture inspired of God is also profitable...."
Thus the translators tamper with the inspiration of the Bible.

Listen, my friend, Jesus said in Luke 21:33, "Heaven and
earth shall pass away: but my words shall not pass away."
You hear me today, Heaven and earth, this earth and the

heavens may pass away, but Jesus said, "My Word never will pass away."

I feel in my soul that even in fundamental, Bible-believing churches such as this one, there are people who are wavering on whether or not the Bible means what it says. We have just been laughed at enough and ridiculed enough and called old-fashioned long enough that some fundamental people are wavering a little on whether or not the Bible is the Word of God. Peter got the message that day. He wrote of it in his epistles later.

John got the message. In John 10:35, which John wrote years later, Jesus says, "The scripture cannot be broken." I sure am glad of that! The Scripture cannot be broken; not one verse of the Bible can ever be broken. You say, "What does that mean?" Well, this Book is the final court of appeals on what we believe and how we live.

We have come to the day when Christian people will look at you and say, "Yes, I know the Bible says that, *but....*" I don't know how a Christian can use that language. "Yes, I know the Bible says that, but..., *but* I think...; I know the Bible says that, *but* I am going to do so and so." Listen; whatever this Book says is God's Holy Word and a Christian's conduct is to be conformed to the Bible. This is the fulfillment of prophecy.

"And was transfigured before them...."—Matt. 17:2.

II. I See in the Transfiguration of Jesus the Wonderful Power of Prayer

Look at Luke 9:28,29: "He took Peter and John and James, and went up into a mountain to pray." (Why did He take those three; and why did He leave the other nine at the foot of the mountain?) "And as he prayed, the fashion of his countenance was altered...." The word here is "altered"; and the word "transfigured" means "changed." As Jesus prayed, His countenance was changed.

You find more than one man in the Bible whose very countenance, whose very looks were changed by the power of prayer. Moses spent forty days and forty nights on top of the mountain and in fellowship with God, while God spoke to him and revealed to him the law. When Moses came down from that mountaintop, his face shined. Exodus 34:29 says, "And it came to pass, when Moses came down from mount Sinai with the two tables of testimony in Moses' hand, when he came down from the mount, that Moses wist not that the skin of his face shone while he talked with him." People could see it; Moses couldn't.

There is a lesson here. Whenever you meet a person who has to tell you that he has been in prayer, and he has to tell you he has been fasting, and when he comes with a long, sober face and says, "I have been in prayer and fasting," that is not the most acceptable thing. One who has been with God will come forth with a shining face. He won't know it but the people will.

Old Moses came from the mountaintop after forty days of fellowship with God with a shining face.

Many of God's people do not have what I would call a shining face. I am afraid that there are not many people who are enjoying their salvation. Let me tell you, when you come to the house of God and hear the good old gospel singing and the preaching of the Word of God, your face ought to light up like a lamp. We, of all people, should be the happiest people in the world. God have mercy on a church filled with Christians who never know how to say AMEN! Sometimes I feel I have to do all of the preaching and the "amen-ing," too.

Oh, listen; a shining face is important. Old Stephen had one. "And all that sat in the council, looking stedfastly on him, saw his face as it had been the face of an angel" (Acts 6:15). That man, one of the first deacons, had such communion with God in prayer that we read of him that "all that sat in the council, looking stedfastly on him, saw his face as it had been the face of an angel." Boy! I have looked in the faces of some Christians that reminded me of but one angel—the fallen angel! Old Stephen's face looked like an angel's. Why? Because he had been in the presence of God.

Paul was writing about that in II Corinthians 3:18, "But we all, with open face beholding as in a glass the glory of the Lord, are changed into the same image from glory to glory, even as by the Spirit of the Lord." Oh, the way to be changed and transformed and transfigured is to go to God and stay in His presence until you get a holy glow in your face.

So here I see the power of prayer. Now, listen; I have never believed a preacher ought to preach any better than he lives. The hardest thing in the world is for a preacher to live like he preaches. It is hard for us to live like we talk. The Bible says, "...of all that Jesus began both to do and teach" (Acts 1:1). His doing and His teaching went hand in hand. That is never true of anybody else.

I wouldn't want to try to impress you in any way in the world, but I can say humbly and with deep conviction in my soul that the past twelve months of my life in the service of the Lord have convinced me as no other twelve months have, that the power of prayer is the greatest instrument in the hands of God. If you don't like someone, pray for him. If you don't like a situation, pray about it. If you don't have what you need, ask for it. If you want more of God's power, pray about it. Oh, the power of prayer! If Jesus, the Son of God, could climb a snow-capped mountain and wait upon God until His very face was changed, so can we.

I see here the power of prayer. I just believe that prayer will change anything or anybody. Oh, how we need to pray, pray, pray, until the victory comes, and pray until you know God has done something for your soul.

"And was transfigured before them...."—Matt. 17:2.

_III. I Feel a Personal Love Demonstrated

People today need to know that God loves them. I am not

talking about unsaved people but saved people. A lot of saved people act as if God has quit loving them. I read that Jesus took "Peter, James, and John." Why? I can't honestly say that He loved them any more than He loved the other nine, but there was some reason why Jesus took "Peter, James, and John." Let's see if we can find why. Three times He took them and left nine behind.

He took them that day He went into the room where the twelve-year-old girl lay dead. He was going to raise her to life, so He took "Peter, James, and John." Wouldn't you like to have seen that? Oh, I wish I could have seen Jesus when He reached and took that little cold hand of that twelve-year-old girl and said, "Damsel, I say unto thee, arise" (Mark 5:41). She that was dead sat up. I wish I could have seen the face of that mother when she saw her daughter move, as she started toward her with open arms. I wish I could have seen that tenderhearted father standing in that room when he saw his own flesh and blood brought to life. Peter, James, and John got to see it.

When Jesus went that night into the awful agony of the Garden of Gethsemane, when He wrestled with death and Hell as He never did on another occasion except on the cross, He took Peter, James, and John. Out there on that big rock, with blood flowing from the pores of His brow, crying from His broken heart, "O my Father, if it be possible, let this cup pass from me: nevertheless not as I will, but as thou wilt," three men were present in it all, Peter, James, and John. Why these three?

That day when He looked toward the summit of the Mount of Transfiguration and knew that on that mountaintop would come the most glorious picture that men could ever see, He took "Peter, James, and John." Why? Now, I am sure that I don't know all the answers but I think I know some.

Let's take them one by one. Why would He take Peter? In that sixteenth chapter of Matthew, the chapter that tells of Jesus looking at those twelve and asking them one of the greatest theological questions that could ever be asked, "Whom do men say that I the Son of man am?" He spoke of His identity. They said, "Some say that thou art John the Baptist: some, Elias; and others, Jeremias, or one of the prophets." (Now, you wait just a minute, brother; there is something there. He is going to prove to them in a little while that He was not Moses nor Elijah.) He said, "Whom do men say that I...am?" They said, 'Some say that You are Moses, some say that You are Elijah, some Jeremiah; some just say that You are one of the prophets.' Jesus asked them, "But whom say ye that I am?"

Simon Peter spoke up and said, "Thou art the Christ, the Son of the living God" (Matt. 16:16). Simon Peter said, "I know who You are." Jesus said, "Blessed art thou, Simon Bar-jona: for flesh and blood hath not revealed it unto thee, but my Father which is in heaven" (Matt. 16:17). Simon Peter, of all the twelve, says, "I know who You are." Jesus said, "Thou art Peter [small stone] and upon this rock [solid stone, Himself] I will build my church." Here is a man who was later used to play a most important role in the Christian church, Simon Peter. He even preached the sermon on the day of Pentecost. He took the Gospel to the Gentiles for the first time. When Jesus was going to the mountaintop to give a picture of His coming glory, He said, "Peter, I want you to come with Me." I think that is why He took Peter.

Why did He take James? Read Acts 12 and you will find that not too long after this there were two men in jail — Peter and James. The church prayed and God answered, and Peter got released. But Acts 12 says that they took a sword and cut off James' head. Jesus knew that was going to happen. That day when He thought of His coming glory and saw a picture of resurrected saints in new, glorified, heavenly bodies, Jesus perhaps said, "James, it will not be long until your head will be severed from your body. I want you to see this picture. Come with Me."

Why did He take John? When we come to the twenty-seven books of the New Testament, we find that this man was used of God to write five tremendously important books: the Gospel of John, the three epistles of John, and the greatest book on prophecy ever written, the book of the Revelation. John was to write those five books inspired of God. Jesus, when He got ready to go to the summit conference where there would be a picture of Him and all coming glory, said, "John, I think you ought to see it."

He took Peter, James, and John, and they never forgot that hour. Of all the events that they ever saw—the miracles wrought, the sermons preached, the dead raised—they never got over the transfiguration. Years later they wrote of it. Simon Peter said in his second epistle, chapter 1, verse 16: "For we have not followed cunningly devised fables, when we made known unto you the power and coming of our Lord Jesus Christ, but were eyewitnesses of his majesty." Years later, Simon Peter wrote on the second coming, "I am not talking to you about a cunningly devised fable, but I am telling you what my eyes have seen."

John wrote of it in John 1:14, "And the Word was made flesh, and dwelt among us, (and we beheld his glory, the glory as of the only begotten of the Father,)...." That is why He took them and He loved them. He loved Simon Peter, He loved James, who was going to die. He loved old John, who was going to spend his last years as an old gray-haired man on a little rocky island out in the sea, and tradition says he was boiled in oil until he died. Jesus loved him. He said, "I want you to see Me in all of My glory. Then when the trials and tribulations come, you will know how to take it."

Oh, let men hate me if they must, but I have a Christ of God whom I know loves me! John 13:1, "...having loved his own which were in the world, he loved them unto the end." He'll never quit loving me.

"And was transfigured before them...."—Matt. 17:2.

IV. I See a Picture of Christ's Return

Now let us see this scene up there. Let us get the picture in our minds. As Peter, James, John, and Jesus reached the mountaintop, they began to pray. The heavens burst with the glory of God; and two heavenly visitors came. Thus on that mountaintop were six men. Let us see the picture on the mountaintop. There are five pictures just as plain and clear as they will be when the Lord comes.

First of all, there is the Lord glorified. They said His countenance was changed. They said His hair was white like snow. He stood in the snow, we suppose, if the Mount of Transfiguration were Mount Hermon, for this mountaintop twelve months of the year is never without snow. I looked one day and saw that snow-capped mountain and said to the guide, "How far away is it?" (It looked like three or four miles.) He said, "It's sixty miles." There it stood just as clear as if it were across the way a little distance.

Jesus was standing in the snow perhaps when they saw Him glorified. They saw Him as John saw Him. John said, "...his eyes were as a flame of fire...his feet like unto fine brass...and his voice as the sound of many waters." They saw the glorified Christ.

I thank God I am going to see Him one day. I am going to see Him, bless God, and when I do, I am going to belong to Him. I won't have to be afraid. I'll be one of His, and I am going to be like Him.

They saw the glorified Jesus and they saw something else, too. They saw Moses. There is something about Moses I like. Moses lived 120 years and, the Bible says, his strength was not abated. One day God said to Moses, "The children of Israel are going over into Canaan but you can't go because you lost your temper that day and smote the rock when I said to speak to the rock." If God should keep out of Heaven everyone who had lost his temper one time, that would settle it for me and, I suppose, for most of you. But He said to Moses, "You may see the land but you're not going to lead them in." Then old Moses climbed Mount Pisgah in the Nebo range of mountains, and when he got on Pisgah's mountaintop, he looked over and there it was—the land that for forty years he had prayed to get to. God said, "You can't go in. You are going to die up here."

Moses had a funeral the like of which no one else has ever had. He died, but what a funeral! Do you know who conducted his funeral? God did. God called a special angel by the name of Michael (read it in Jude 9), and God said to Michael, one of the three archangels, "Michael, I want you to take him and bury him somewhere in this mountain, and I want nobody ever to know where he is buried." I don't know why. Perhaps if the Catholics had known where he was buried, they would have got him and put him in the Vatican. Maybe the Lord knew that, and that is one reason He didn't want anybody to know. I think maybe the Lord never wanted him to be worshiped. So God said, "Nobody is going to know where I bury him."

Jude 9 tells us that there was a dispute between Michael the archangel of God and the Devil over the body of Moses. The Devil wanted to get it and keep it and preserve it and make an image of it, as they did to the brazen serpent and many other things, but God said that nobody would ever know.

Moses appeared on that mountaintop, and the disciples knew that one day he had lain down, at the age of 120, and died, and that he was buried in that mountain; yet there he was in Palestine! That is a picture of the resurrection. It may be just a doctrine to you, but may God make it real to you. The saints which sleep in Him will Jesus bring with Him when He comes again. He is going to raise the dead. I like that. "For if [since] we believe that Jesus died and rose again, even so them also which sleep in Jesus will God bring with him" (I Thess. 4:14).

I think I shall tell you about getting some cemetery lots the other day. They came to me in a strange and unusual way and I am not able to tell you about it. But I stood out in the middle of the place where they think I am going to be buried, if the Lord tarries; but I can't see myself out there. It's just not like me! It really isn't. I'm like Brother Lester Roloff, who said, "If I ever die, it's going to be one great surprise to me." I feel the same way! I can't see it. I never would let anybody lock me up in anything. There are not enough men in here to lock me up in a telephone booth. I don't want to be locked up in anything, and I don't think I ever will allow anybody to lock me in something. I can't see myself out there. But a lot of us here have loved ones who have gone.

When Peter, James, and John saw Moses, they said, "Yes, bless God, it's real!" We may die but the Lord is going to bring us back to life, and that will take place when Jesus comes.

They saw another man, Elijah. And by the way, Moses and Elijah represent all the law and all the prophets. They saw Elijah and you know Elijah didn't die. Elijah was translated, as the Old Testament tells us. He never died. He walked along one day and while Elisha was with him, the heavens were filled with the chariots of God and fire came down, and after a while Elijah went up to Heaven without dying; thus he becomes a picture of the translated saints who will never die.

Paul spoke of this in I Corinthians 15:51, "Behold, I shew you a mystery; We shall not all sleep...." We use the old expression "as sure as death and taxes." Now taxes are pretty sure but death is not certain. "We shall not all sleep, but shall all be changed, In a moment, in the twinkling of an eye...." Somebody said the twinkling of an eye is the length of time after the red light turns green until the woman in the car behind blows her horn for you to move on! It will not take long—just the snap of a finger. "In a moment, in the twinkling of an eye...the dead shall be raised

..." (I Cor. 15:52), and we are going to be translated if we are living when He comes.

I see another picture here of Peter, James, and John. There's a picture of the coming of the Lord represented in the Jewish remnant who are going to be alive and loving Him and mourning, as Zechariah says, for Him to come, and looking for Him. I thank God for Jewish people who are saved and baptized. A converted Jew shook hands with me and said, "I want to serve the Lord, and anything I can do for the church and for Jesus, I want to do it." I thank God He can save a Jew. And there are a few saved.

Now I see a fifth picture here and it is a picture of the multitude down at the foot of the mountain, who represent the vast millions of people who are lost and will be lost when Jesus comes. Only those that we get to with the Gospel will be saved.

"And [Jesus] *was transfigured before them...."*—Matt. 17:2.

V. The Preeminence of Jesus

It is here like it is everywhere in the Bible. Notice this expression, "Jesus only." "They saw no man, save Jesus only" (Matt. 17:8). Notice this expression: God said, "Hear ye him." Listen to Him! "Jesus only." Hear Him (Col. 1:18), "that in all things he might have the preeminence."

God the Father, God the Holy Spirit, the blessed Word of God always give the preeminence to Jesus. When He was born it was not Mary or angels but Jesus who had the glory. "For unto you is born this day in the city of David a Saviour, which is Christ the Lord" (Luke 2:11).

When He was baptized it was not John the Baptist nor the ordinance of baptism which was given the preeminence but the Lord Jesus Himself. "And Jesus, when he was baptized, went up straightway out of the water: and, lo, the heavens were opened unto him, and he saw the Spirit of God descending like a dove, and lighting upon him: And lo, a voice from heaven, saying, This is my beloved Son in whom I am well pleased" (Matt. 3:16,17).

When He died upon the cross of Calvary, God glorified Him. It was not the thieves who died or the rabble who crucified Him or the religious leaders who were prominent, but Jesus it was who was exalted. The hours of darkness, the rending of the veil, the resurrection of the saints, the rending of the rocks, all declared what the centurion said: "Truly this was the Son of God" (Matt. 27:54).

So on the Mount of Transfiguration Jesus was preeminent.

"And [He] *was transfigured before them...."—Matt. 17:2.*

VI. I See Peter's Forgetting the Lost Multitude

I wish I had saved more time for this part of the message. Peter forgot the multitude at the foot of the mountain. He said, "Lord, it's so good here! Let's just stay here." I am told that in the Greek it didn't say, "...let us build," but "I will build three booths, or three tabernacles, one for you, one for Moses and one for Elijah." I guess he thought it was so good being up there with this going on and separated from sin and evil and the lost, that he and James and John would stay outside; I don't know why. He said, "three tabernacles."

Peter forgot something—he forgot the multitude down there at the foot of the mountain. That is what a lot of you have forgotten. You are a Christian, you are saved, you have a church, you have a Christian home, but you have forgotten that there are hundreds of people who are lost. It has been weeks and months (maybe never) since some of you walked down an aisle and led a sinner to Jesus Christ. You forgot the same thing Peter did—that there is a multitude at the foot of the mountain who need God and will never know Him unless you go to them.

He forgot something else. Peter got things twisted around, and I believe he wanted the crown without the cross. He said, "Since we are already here, let's just stay. If You go back there, like You say, You are going to die and we are going to die, too, as You have told us. We are going to be persecuted! Lord, let's stay up here and let's wait for the glorious kingdom, and let's not have any crosses."

Listen! I don't know of a picture in the Bible that is more accurate of the Christians than this. They want the crown but don't want any cross. They want the easy way. They do not want to sacrifice; they do not want to be inconvenienced. O God, have mercy on the Christians of this day who want a crown and no cross!

I am glad that I saw this in the Bible because it came to me when I needed it. There is a cross for all of us. People lie about you (and I don't want anybody's sympathy; God knows that). I've poked fun at folks who always go around bragging on preachers and sympathizing with them. I don't want that, and so I don't say it for that reason; but I have never been lied about and lied on and lied to as much as I have lately. I have never seen so much rebellion against God's leadership as I have seen in the past few weeks.

The other day I got to feeling kind of sorry for myself and I thought, "Lord, I'm trying to do right, trying to preach the Word of God and do the work, so why should anybody hate me?" I got to feeling kind of sorry for myself. Then I read this, and the thought came to me, Bless God! before the crown comes the cross! "If any man will come after me, let him deny himself, and take up his cross daily, and follow me" (Luke 9:23).

Do you know why Jesus took these three up there? He wanted them to know that beyond the cross and when you get to the crown (pardon my grammer!), it ain't going to be half bad!

And He knew that after that hour on that mountaintop, the cross would be lighter. Some of you have a cross; haven't you? It gets awfully heavy and sometimes it makes you weak and it makes you want to give up. But remember, before the crown comes the cross, and after the cross comes the crown.

It is like those two sisters: one got saved and the other was lost. That night the lost sister dressed up in her evening gown and dancing slippers, and she stood before the mirror while the other one read her Bible. The lost sister was pinning in her hair a piece of jewelry that glittered and shined, while her sister lay across the bed with the Word of God.

The unsaved girl said, "Look what you have, an old-fashioned Book! Look at these nice clothes and glittering jewelry. I'm going to have a good time!"

It is said that the Christian girl raised up from her Book and with a smile that could only come from God, said, "Some day I'll wear a crown that will outshine that a million to one," and went back to her reading.

After the cross, comes the crown.

"And [Jesus] *was transfigured before them...."*—*Matt. 17:2.*

VII. They Talked of His Death

Now the last wonderful thing: What did they talk about? Moses talked and Elijah talked. Jesus talked. Simon Peter talked a little, but he never should have said a word; he didn't know about that verse that Paul wrote later, "Study to be quiet." The Bible plainly said that he didn't know what to say, so he just had to blab out something. That is what some of you do. You don't know what to do nor what to say, so you just blab out something. It is nearly always wrong when you talk that way.

But Moses and Elijah talked and Jesus talked, but what did they talk about. Here's the Summit Conference. Two men from Glory—one had been dead 1500 years and the other had been gone 900 years—they come back, one 1500 years, one 900 years. There they are. What did they talk about? The Bible says they "spoke of His decease which He would accomplish at Jerusalem." They talked about His death. Jesus turned to the twelve (in Matthew 16) and said, "I'm going to die." Peter said, "Far be it from you, Lord," And Jesus had to rebuke him with "get thee behind me, Satan: for thou savourest not the things that be of God, but the things that be of men" (Mark 8:33).

When Jesus talked to the twelve of His death, He got no sympathy. Old Moses said, "Yes, I know you're going to die, Jesus. I've been believing that for 1500 years. I believed it that night when I took the Passover lamb and filled the basin with blood and sprinkled it on the lintel and on the doorposts. I believed in the death of Jesus when I saw the blood run from the lintel down to the floor. When I sprinkled it on both sides and looked back and there was a bloody cross, I knew You were going to die. I knew it that night when I laid the little lamb on the altar and put the knife to its throat, shed its blood, and burned its little body with fire. I was thinking of Calvary then. I knew You were going to die, Jesus. I knew it that day when they were bitten with the fiery serpents and were dying by the thousands, and I lifted up the serpent of brass; I knew when I lifted it up that it was a glorious picture of a type of the Son of God, who would take away the sins of the world, who would come and die. I know You are going to die."

You will pardon me, because I do not mean to be irreverent, but I think it encouraged Jesus. Jesus said, "All right, let's go back down the mountainside."

As they walked down the mountainside, He said, "For the time being, don't tell anybody what happened because they will never believe you, but later on they will."

Yes, at the foot of the mountain was a multitude who needed to hear the message of Calvary. There was a brokenhearted father and a son for whom there was no hope outside of Jesus Christ. There was a group of powerless Christians with no answer to human needs. Christ is the answer to every heart cry, every human need. He is the

Saviour of sinners and the friend of lost people. He is God's answer to sin.   May God help you to believe on Him as your Saviour.

"And they said, Believe on the Lord Jesus Christ, and thou shalt be saved, and thy house."—Acts 16:31.

"And [Jesus] *was transfigured before them...."*—Matt. 17:2.

THE TRIUMPHANT ENTRY OF JESUS CHRIST

"And the multitudes that went before, and that followed, cried, saying, Hosanna to the son of David: Blessed is he that cometh in the name of the Lord; Hosanna in the highest."—Matt. 21:9.

  I. To Fulfill Bible Prophecy

 II. To Prove He Was the Creator and Owner of All Things

III. To Die for the Sins of the World

IV. To Be Betrayed by a Friend

 V. To Show His Matchless Humility

VI. To Arise From the Dead

VII. That People Might Know They Could Be Saved

The Golden Gate in the Wall of Jerusalem

"And when he was come nigh, even now at the descent of the mount of Olives, the whole multitude of the disciples began to rejoice and praise God...Saying, Blessed be the King that cometh in the name of the Lord...." - Luke 19:37,38.

5

The Triumphant Entry of Jesus Christ

"And the multitudes that went before, and that followed, cried, saying, Hosanna to the son of David: Blessed is he that cometh in the name of the Lord; Hosanna in the highest."—Matt. 21:9.

The Sunday before Easter Sunday is called Palm Sunday. There are some days that the church for centuries has observed which are not particularly biblical and scriptural. That is not the case, however, with what we call Palm Sunday. It is the Sunday before the resurrection of Jesus Christ. It is scripturally called Palm Sunday because in John 12:13, we read that they broke palm branches from the trees and lined the streets in front of Jesus Christ as He made His triumphant entry into the city of Jerusalem. "Much people...took branches of palm trees, and went forth to meet him, and cried, Hosanna: Blessed is the King of Israel that cometh in the name of the Lord."

The Scripture that I have read to you probably describes Jesus' most popular hour. There were many times, you know, when Jesus was not popular. There were even times, you know, when He was misunderstood by His own. Much of the earthly life of Jesus Christ was spent alone. But here is one of those moments in His earthly ministry that has been called by many His most popular hour.

We read that on this occasion a great multitude said, "Who is this?" (Matt. 21:10). We read that even the enemies of Jesus said, "...the world is gone after him" (John 12:19).

The occasion was Palm Sunday, one week before His resurrection from the grave. Jesus had said to His disciples, in a little village called Bethphage that nestled around the base of the Mount of Olives, 'Go to a certain corner where two ways meet; there will be a home. You will find a colt tied; bring that beast of burden. I am going to ride it into the city today.'

They did as they were told and they brought this little donkey and they put their garments upon it and they sat Jesus upon the little animal. Jesus rides down from the side of the Mount of Olives and through the Garden of Gethsemane, and goes through what is called the Golden Gate, entering from the east side into the city of old Jerusalem.

Down the streets He goes and the multitudes literally pack the city. They cry out, "Who is this?" The answer is, "This is Jesus the prophet of Nazareth of Galilee" (Matt. 21:11). The Pharisees stood back and said on this occasion, "There are so many people acclaiming Jesus Christ that it looks like the whole world has gone after Him." This is called His presentation of Himself as King. I like to think of it as "The Triumphant Entry of Jesus Christ."

This is the beginning of His last week on earth. Packed into these six days, before He arises from the grave, there will happen the greatest spiritual events that ever took place on earth.

First of all, during this time Jesus will institute the Lord's Supper that teaches His blood atonement, His death upon Calvary, and His second coming in the clouds of Glory. Every believer ought to carefully study I Corinthians 11:23-34.

During these next few days you will see Him yonder under an old olive tree, perhaps lying prostrate across a huge stone. In the moonlight of the night before His death upon the cross, you will hear Him say, "O my Father, if it be possible, let this cup pass from me." The travail of His soul will cause great drops of blood to ooze from every pore of His body.

During this week, you will see the blackest hand of human history. You will see a man dip a piece of bread with Him in the dish, one who is to betray Him for thirty pieces of silver.

During this week you will see the greatest farce of justice that the world has ever known. You will see Jesus undergo two trials—a religious trial and a civil trial, both of which will go down in the annals of human history as the greatest injustice ever perpetrated on the face of the earth. It is during these six days that are to follow this triumphant entry that you will see them take Him and number Him with two malefactors. And with a heavy cross they will take Him to Calvary. On that little, barren, rocky, skull-shaped hill they shall lift Him up between Heaven and earth, robed in blood and crowned with thorns, as if too unclean for earth and not fit for Heaven.

It is during this next week the most important thing will happen that you will ever read of in the Bible. The stone will be rolled away from the sepulchre that held His blessed body, and He will shake the graveclothes and triumphantly walk out of the tomb. This triumphant entry of Jesus Christ is the beginning of the greatest week in all history.

I have asked myself this question: Why did Jesus, the Sunday before His resurrection Sunday, parade into the city amidst the acclaim of multiplied thousands? I believe there are seven reasons:

1. To fulfill Bible prophecy;
2. To prove He was the Creator and Owner of all things;
3. To die for the sins of the world;
4. To be betrayed by a friend;
5. To show His matchless humility;
6. To arise from the dead;
7. That people might know they could be saved.

Jesus made His triumphant entry

I. To Fulfill Bible Prophecy

In the first place, He did it to fulfill Bible prophecy.

Jesus was careful to see that everything that was supposed to be fulfilled concerning Himself literally came to pass. Even when dying upon the cross, Jesus had such an earnest devotion to this Word that He realized that there was one thing that had not yet been fulfilled, and that was that when He died He would ask for water. And so on the cross He cried, "I thirst" (John 19:28), that the Word of God might be fulfilled and that Scripture might never be broken.

Five hundred years before Jesus was born of a virgin, the prophet Zechariah took up his prophetical trumpet and began to blow. You read where he recorded this incident in the ministry of Jesus Christ when, riding upon the back of a humble little donkey, He would go into the city amidst the acclaim of many thousands of people. Zechariah 9:9 says: "Rejoice greatly, O daughter of Zion; shout, O daughter of Jerusalem: behold, thy King cometh unto thee: he is just, and having salvation; lowly, and riding upon an ass, and upon a colt the foal of an ass."

You see, five hundred years before this ever took place the Bible said that He would enter the city riding a donkey and the foal of an ass. The Bible said thousands would acclaim Him and would cry, "Hosanna in the highest." That is exactly what took place. And they asked, "Who is this?"

I wish I had time to answer that question this morning, "Who is this, that they throw their clothes in the streets for Him to ride upon? Who is this that causes them to cry, 'Behold our King'?"

Who is this? This is the Lamb of the Old Testament. This is the Rock smitten by Moses. This is the Ark built by Noah. This is the Well of Salvation, the King of kings, the Saviour of the world. This is the Son of God. He fulfills Bible prophecy.

"And the multitudes that went before, and that followed, cried, saying, Hosanna to the son of David: Blessed is he that cometh in the name of the Lord; Hosanna in the highest."—Matt. 21:9.

II. To Prove He Was the Creator and Owner of All Things

Jesus went into the city on Palm Sunday to prove that He was the Creator and Owner of all things. There is a beautiful truth here. I believe it has been overlooked many times by those of us who love the Bible. He said, "Go into the village over against you, and straightway ye shall find an ass tied, and a colt with her: loose them, and bring them unto me" (Matt. 21:2).

Jesus said to two disciples, 'I want you to go to a certain place and there will be a little beast of burden with its mother. I want you to bring them to Me.' They did not belong to the disciples. In the human scheme of things, they did not actually belong to the Lord Jesus Christ. But He said, 'Bring them to Me.'

These two disciples evidently said to Jesus, "But suppose someone says to us, 'These do not belong to you. You have no right to take them.'"

Jesus said, 'If anyone questions you, you say to them that the Lord hath need of them, and that will settle it.'

So, the disciples went and when the owner saw them taking the mother and the little donkey, he said, "Why are you taking these?"

The disciples answered, "The Lord hath need of them." In other words, "These belong to God, the Creator of the world, who made life, who created everything. He has sent for these."

Jesus demonstrates here that everything, everything in this world, without a single exception, belongs to God Almighty. You know many a person has forgotten this great truth: "The earth is the Lord's, and the fulness thereof," that He made all things by the word of His mouth and that He upholds them by the power of His hands. He demonstrates here on Palm Sunday that He is the Owner and the Creator of everything in this world.

You know, everything obeys the Lord except one thing.

One day God said to a big fish, "Swallow a preacher." He did! One day God said to a donkey upon whom Balaam rode, "Speak to your master." He did! One day Jesus said to a little rooster, "At a certain time, I want you to crow to teach one of my preachers a lesson in repentance."

I can just see that little old rooster when Peter had backslidden and failed the Lord. He gets up bright and early, long before daybreak, gets up on a fence and flaps his wings, stretches his little neck and limbers his throat. Maybe the Lord said, "Now wait a minute, rooster; I am not quite ready." After a while he started to crow again and He said, "Just a minute now." After a while, the little rooster lets loose, because Jesus told him to do it. You see, everything —the fish in the sea, the birds in the air—everything obeys God, except one thing. That is man. Man is the only one that ever grieved Him. Man is the only one that ever disobeyed Him. Everything, human beings included, belongs to God Almighty.

The Lord has a twofold hold on everyone in this building this morning. "All things were made by him; and without him was not any thing made that was made" (John 1:3).

I read a story that I believe illustrates this in a wonderful way. A little boy had made a boat and was sailing his little boat, tied to a string, in the stream. It is said that the string broke and the boat went out of his sight, and he lost it. He had spent a lot of time on it and it was a beautiful piece of work.

One day, not long afterwards, as he was walking down the streets of his city he saw that little boat sitting in the window of an antique shop. So the little boy went into that shop and said to the man, "That is my boat."

The man said, "I bought that boat from someone. It belongs to me. It doesn't belong to you."

The little boy said, "I made that boat and I lost it a day or two ago. That boat was made by my own hands. It belongs to me."

The man said, "No, it is mine, not yours. If you want it, you will have to buy it."

The little boy pulled the asking price of two or three dollars out of his pocket, handed it to the man, took the little boat, stuck it under his arm, and walked down the sidewalk on his way back to his home. As he did, he was heard to say, "Little boat, you belong to me for two reasons. You belong to me, first of all, because I made you. You belong to me now because I bought you."

My friends, you belong to God because you are made in His image. You belong to God because He bought you with the price of His blood upon the cross of Calvary. You are His rightfully, in a twofold way.

"And the multitudes that went before, and that followed, cried, saying, Hosanna to the son of David: Blessed is he that cometh in the name of the Lord; Hosanna in the highest."—Matt. 21:9.

III. To Die for the Sins of the World

In the third place, Jesus entered the city of Jerusalem to die for the sins of the world.

Long before this, Jesus had told His disciples "how that he must go unto Jerusalem, and suffer many things of the elders and chief priests and scribes, and be killed, and be raised again the third day" (Matt. 16:21). Here is all this crowd and here are these disciples, and Jesus had said to them, 'I am going to Jerusalem to die, not to be made King. I am going to Jerusalem to die for the sins of the world.' Yet, on this occasion, everyone forgot it. The multitude wanted to acclaim Him King. Not one disciple said, "This is not the purpose. You must die on the cross." In fact, Simon Peter said to Him one day, "Jesus, You don't need to die and You don't need to be crucified." Jesus said, "Get thee behind me, Satan: for thou savourest not the things that be of God, but the things that be of men" (Mark 8:33).

The purpose for Jesus' going to Jerusalem was to die on the cross for the sins of the world.

Jesus talked to Nicodemus that night on the streets of Jerusalem, and Nicodemus was religious but lost. He said to Nicodemus, "As Moses lifted up the serpent in the wilderness, even so must the Son of man be lifted up: That whosoever believeth in him should not perish, but have eternal life. For God so loved the world, that he gave his only begotten Son, that whosoever believeth in him should not perish, but have everlasting life" (John 3:14-16). He said, 'Nicodemus, the Son of man MUST be lifted up. Just as Moses lifted up the serpent, so God will lift up His Son.' That is the purpose of Jesus' coming to earth.

He mentioned it in John 12:32,33: "And I, if I be lifted up from the earth, will draw all men unto me. This he said, signifying what death he should die." I say to you, there is no more important teaching that ever came from the lips of man than the substitutionary, vicarious death, the bloody death of Jesus Christ upon the cross. It is the absolute proof, beyond any shadow of a doubt, of God's love for you and me. Romans 5:8 says, "But God commendeth his love toward us, in that, while we were yet sinners, Christ died for us." Why did He go to Jerusalem? To die for the sins of the world.

"And the multitudes that went before, and that followed, cried, saying, Hosanna to the son of David: Blessed is he that cometh in the name of the Lord; Hosanna in the highest."—Matt. 21:9.

IV. To Be Betrayed by a Friend

He went, in the fourth place, to be betrayed by a friend. I have preached whole sermons on the betrayal by Judas of Jesus Christ. There are some important lessons to be learned by it. Matthew 26:21 says, "And as they did eat, he said, Verily I say unto you, that one of you shall betray me." There is a play on words." "Not the multitude, not the thousands who outwardly hate Me, not those who have sought to stone Me and kill Me prior to this—but one of YOU shall betray Me. Not those out there who have placed no faith in Me, but one of you. One of you who have been with Me three years; one of you who have heard all of My teaching; one of you who have seen all My miracles; one of you who know there is no fraud to be found in Me: one of you shall betray Me."

They began to question Jesus. "Lord, is it I? Lord, is it I?" Jesus said, "He that dippeth his hand with me in the dish, the same shall betray me."

In the most spiritual hour of the public ministry of Jesus Christ, when the Lord's Supper is instituted, the blackest hand of human history reached in the dish and Jesus said, 'THIS is the one.' One of those twelve, a preacher, sold the Son of God and arose and went out. The Bible says it was night; and it always will be night in the heart and mind of one who has sold the Son of God. "One of YOU shall betray me."

He mentioned it in John, chapter 6, when multitudes came, when He said, "Have not I chosen you twelve, and one of you is a devil?" The next verse says, "He spake of Judas Iscariot the son of Simon: for he it was that should betray him, being one of the twelve" (John 6:71). He said, 'I have CHOSEN you twelve. I chose Judas Iscariot, I selected him, I called him, I sent him; but I chose him, knowing that he would betray me.'

You say to me, "Preacher, why would Jesus Christ choose a man that He knew would never be saved? Why would He choose a man who would go out preaching and on healing campaigns, yet never know the Lord? Why did He choose Judas Iscariot?"

He chose him to fulfill the Scripture. He chose him to provide one of the most impartial witnesses Jesus ever had. For in the hours that followed, old Judas came, and that money, still burning heart, hands, and conscience, he flung down at the feet of those who gave it to him and said, "I have sinned in that I have betrayed the innocent blood."

He chose Judas to be an impartial witness to His innocence. He chose Judas to prove the ever-presence of hypocrisy and insincerity and the ever-presence of religion without salvation.

I am positive that there are hundreds and hundreds of church members who have never been born again, yet they are religious. You say that is hard to believe. But here is a man who was with Jesus three years. He slept with Him at night, ate with Him at the table; he heard all of Jesus' teaching, saw all of His miracles, watched Him raise the dead, but was never born again! He was religious but lost. He was a hypocrite in his apostolate.

Jesus' tolerance of Judas was one of the greatest examples of tolerance ever shown. For three and a half years He rarely ever mentioned him. For three and a half years He never embarrassed him. For three and a half years, until the end time came, Jesus let him alone and watched him, knowing that Judas would sell Him some day.

My friends, if there is anything God's people, and even unsaved people, are going to need more of in the days to come and in the crucial hour in which we live, it is a tolerant heart and a tolerant spirit. If Jesus Christ could forgive one who sold Him for thirty pieces of silver, it behooves every Christian to forgive those who have wronged him.

I am amazed at the tolerance of Jesus. That night in the garden, Judas came and said, 'Now I will identify Jesus. You will know the One to take and arrest because I am going to kiss the One who is Jesus.' That night in the Garden of Gethsemane, Judas walks up to Jesus, places a kiss upon His brow; and with a kiss he betrayed the precious Son of God. Jesus looked at him and said, "Friend, wherefore art thou come?" The word "friend" in this instance means "comrade." Even in the very moment when Judas was sell-ing Jesus, Jesus said, "Comrade." Oh, the tolerant spirit of Jesus! Even His acts of discipline were done in tender love.

Let me say this to you: If this Bible be true, hatred has no place in the heart of a Christian. Christ and hatred should not live in the same body! You say, "Well, I know people who are saved who are filled with hate." You do not know that they are saved. I repeat: Hatred and Christ should not live in the same body. Jesus was betrayed by a friend.

"And the multitudes that went before, and that followed, cried, saying, Hosanna to the son of David: Blessed is he that cometh in the name of the Lord; Hosanna in the highest."—Matt. 21:9.

V. To Show His Matchless Humility

Oh, see today the Son of God, the Lord of Glory, riding into Jerusalem on the back of a borrowed ass, thronged by the common people. See Him coming down the side of the Mount of Olives weeping over a lost city. "And when he was come near, he beheld the city, and wept over it" (Luke 19: 41).

What matchless humility is here demonstrated by the Lord Jesus Christ! No gilded carriage, no prancing teams of beautiful horses—just a borrowed donkey! Jesus is the greatest living example of humility the world has ever known. "And being found in fashion as a man, he humbled himself, and became obedient unto death, even the death of the cross" (Phil. 2:8).

The Bible teaches that we are to "follow his steps." First Peter 2:21 says, "For even thereunto were ye called: because Christ also suffered for us, leaving us an example, that ye should follow his steps." This surely must mean that we are to humble ourselves as the people of God, in service for Him, in our relationship one to another, and in every respect.

"And the multitudes that went before, and that followed, cried, saying, Hosanna to the son of David: Blessed is he that cometh in the name of the Lord; Hosanna in the highest."—Matt. 21:9.

VI. To Arise From the Dead

In a verse previously quoted, Matthew 16:21, Jesus clearly promised that He would not only die upon a cross but would triumph over the tomb. Oh, what could be said today about the glorious resurrection of our blessed Lord!

I recently stood once again in the beautiful garden near the walls of Jerusalem and beheld the empty tomb. How thrilled I was to be able to say, "He is not here: for he is risen...!" His resurrection guarantees ours!

"Jesus said...I am the resurrection, and the life: he that believeth in me, though he were dead, yet shall he live" (John 11:25).

His resurrection also guarantees our justification. "Who was delivered for our offences, and was raised again for our justification" (Rom. 4:25). It also assures us of a glorious union with those who have gone on before us to the eternal city of God. Thank God for the resurrection!

"And the multitudes that went before, and that followed, cried, saying, Hosanna to the son of David: Blessed is he that cometh in the name of the Lord; Hosanna in the highest."—Matt. 21:9.

VII. That People Might Know They Could Be Saved

Jesus made His triumphant entry into Jerusalem that people might know they could be saved. There is a word here that I believe gives the message all of its meaning. They looked at Jesus that day and the multitudes reached up their hands and cried, "Hosanna! Hosanna! Hosanna!" It is an Old Testament word which means, "Save, we pray!" They looked at Jesus that day and cried, "Jesus, save us!"

Jesus came to do just exactly that. O friend, His triumphant entry was to go to Calvary to die for your sins and mine, that you and I might be saved. Oh, may God speak to your heart! If reading this sermon there is a man or woman, boy or girl who is not a Christian, may you realize that Jesus went to Calvary that you might have everlasting life. "For the Son of man is come to seek and to save that which was lost" (Luke 19:10). "This is a faithful saying, and worthy of all acceptation, that Christ Jesus came into the world to save sinners; of whom I am chief" (I Tim. 1:15).

Yes, Jesus was on His way to Calvary that day when He entered Jerusalem. He had you on His heart and was on His way to take your sins on Himself. In fact, from the beginning of time, Jesus had been going toward Calvary. "And all that dwell upon the earth shall worship him, whose names are not written in the book of life of the Lamb slain from the foundation of the world" (Rev. 13:8). So we see that in the mind and counsel of God, Jesus was slain before ever sun or moon or star or life was made. He was the "Lamb slain from the foundation of the world." He came to save; He lives to keep. He is able to satisfy the deepest need of your life.

"And the multitudes that went before, and that followed, cried, saying, Hosanna to the son of David: Blessed is he that cometh in the name of the Lord; Hosanna in the highest."—Matt. 21:9.

THE SACRIFICIAL DEATH OF JESUS CHRIST

or

THE BIBLE DOCTRINE OF BLOOD ATONEMENT

"The blood of Jesus Christ his Son cleanseth us from all sin."—I John 1:7.

I. The Sacrificial Death of Jesus Was Predetermined

II. The Sacrificial Death of Jesus Was Prophesied

III. The Sacrificial Death of Jesus Christ Means Eternal, Abundant Life to Us

IV. The Blood of Christ Is God's Complete Answer to Sin

V. The Blood of Jesus Is Precious to God and His Church

VI. The Blood of Jesus Is Hated by Satan and Opposed by Modernism

VII. The Blood of Jesus Christ Is the Theme of Heaven's Song

Mount Calvary atop "The Skull"

"And he bearing his cross went forth into a place called the place of a skull, which is called in the Hebrew Golgotha: Where they crucified him."—John 19:17, 18.

6

The Sacrificial Death of Jesus Christ

or
The Bible Doctrine of Blood Atonement

"The blood of Jesus Christ his Son cleanseth us from all sin."—I John 1:7.

Like a never-ending stream, the river of atonement runs from one end of the Bible to the other with increasing width and depth. Every page of sacred writing seems to be stained with the royal scarlet of Jesus' blood. Just as the Bible breathes with inspiration and pulsates with life divine, it bleeds with atoning blood. The sacrificial death of Jesus Christ and His work of redemption is without any shadow of doubt the central theme of the Word of God.

Someone has said that the cordage of the British Navy is identified with a red thread running throughout; so "the scarlet line" of Rahab's faith runs like an ever-widening river of grace from eternity to eternity.

Now when we discuss the doctrine of atonement, we must remember that the word "atonement" itself is entirely an Old Testament Word. It is found once in the English translation of the New Testament.

"And not only so, but we also joy in God through our Lord Jesus Christ, by whom we have now received the atonement."—Rom. 5:11.

The same word translated "atonement" here is translated "reconciliation" in Romans 11:15 and elsewhere. Atonement means "to cover," but the doctrine of blood redemption goes far deeper than that. It includes cleansing, a "blotting out" of our sins, a separation of sin from the sinner, a divine forgiveness, a purchased freedom, and eternal safety of the trusting soul.

Without the incarnation, there would be no Saviour. Without the resurrection of Christ, there would be no assurance. Without the atonement, there would be no forgiveness.

We cannot do without the blood. These today who say, "Away with that slaughterhouse religion," or "no more of that gory story," might as well say, "Lock the gates of Heaven against every hungry heart," because the way of the bloody cross is the only way home to God and His eternal city.

"And almost all things are by the law purged with blood; and without shedding of blood is no remission."—Heb. 9:22.

Some of the great verses of the Bible which have to do with the cleansing blood of Christ have been most influential in my life. Think of such great verses as Leviticus 17:11 which says,

"For the life of the flesh is in the blood: and I have given it to you upon the altar to make an atonement for your souls: for it is the blood that maketh an atonement for the soul."

Also Acts 20:28,

"Take heed therefore unto yourselves, and to all the flock, over the which the Holy Ghost hath made you overseers, to feed the church of God, which he hath purchased with his own blood."

First Peter 1:18,19,

"Forasmuch as ye know that ye were not redeemed with corruptible things, as silver and gold, from your vain conversation received by tradition from your fathers; But with the precious blood of Christ, as of a lamb without blemish and without spot."

I. The Sacrificial Death of Jesus Was Predetermined

We must always remember that the atoning death of Jesus was planned in the eternal councils of God before the beginning of time. His sacrificial death was no afterthought, no accident, no work of man, no spur-of-the-moment strategy of God, but the divine unfolding of God's original and only eternal plan for the salvation of a lost soul. Jesus was not a mere martyr; He was no victim of circumstances; He was no weakling overcome by the viciousness of human depravity. He was the Executor of His own execution; He was both the Offering and the One bringing the offering. He was both the Lamb and the Priest.

"Him, being delivered by the determinate counsel and foreknowledge of God, ye have taken, and by wicked hands have crucified and slain."—Acts 2:23.

"And all that dwell upon the earth shall worship him, whose names are not written in the book of life of the Lamb slain from the foundation of the world."—Rev. 13:8.

Jesus plainly taught in John 10:18 that His death was voluntary.

"No man taketh it from me, but I lay it down of myself. I have power to lay it down, and I have power to take it again. This commandment have I received of my Father."

Before God ever hung the sun or moon or stars in the sky, He planned to give His Son. Before the Spirit of God brooded over the original creation, long before God ever formed man from the dust of the ground, He knew he would need a Saviour and so planned the death of the Son of God.

"The blood of Jesus Christ his Son cleanseth us from all sin."—I John 1:7.

II. The Sacrificial Death of Jesus Was Prophesied

It was prophesied by word. Many, many times God spoke in Old Testament days and declared that in the fullness of time He would send forth His Son.

*"But when the fulness of the time was come, God sent
forth his Son, made of a woman, made under the law, To
redeem them that were under the law, that we might receive the adoption of sons."—Gal. 4:4,5.*

*"And I will put enmity between thee and the woman, and
between thy seed and her seed; it shall bruise thy head, and
thou shalt bruise his heel."—Gen. 3:15.*

There is the seed plot for all the prophesies of the Bible
concerning the coming of a Redeemer. Jesus was the seed
of the woman who was to bruise the head of Satan in the
sacrifice on Calvary.

The 53rd chapter of Isaiah is a great mountain peak of
prophesy concerning the vicarious and sacrificial death of
our Lord Jesus Christ.

*"All we like sheep have gone astray; we have turned every
one to his own way; and the Lord hath laid on him the iniquity of us all. He was oppressed, and he was afflicted, yet
he opened not his mouth: he is brought as a lamb to the
slaughter, and as a sheep before her shearers is dumb, so
he openeth not his mouth."—Isa. 53:6,7.*

The manner of His birth through a virgin was foretold in
Isaiah 7:14; the place where He would be born was foretold
in Micah 5:2; the method by which He would be put to death
was foretold in the 22nd Psalm. The prophets of old took
up their prophetical trumpet and began to sound forth the
thrilling story that Jesus would come from Heaven above to
this unfriendly world to die for the sins of all mankind.

It was prophesied by type. Words cannot describe how
many times God set forth typically the redemption that
would be accomplished by the sacrificial death of Jesus.

I see Jesus in the slain animals whose skins clothed Adam
and Eve.

I see Him in Abel's lamb whose blood was acceptable to
God.

I see Jesus in the ark of Noah as the righteous judgment
of God falls upon it.

I see Him in the passover lamb and the basin of blood.

I see Him in the smitten rock and in the brazen serpent.

I see Jesus in the mercy seat inside the holy of holies. I see Him in every lamb and turtledove and ox offered in the Old Testament.

I see Jesus typically in many persons of the Old Testament. I see Him in Joseph sold by his brethren, in Abraham who offered his son. I see Him in Isaac and David and Daniel. I see Him in the Tabernacle in the wilderness. I see Him and His sacrificial death in every page of the Bible because He said, "Lo, I come (in the volume of the book it is written of me,) to do thy will, O God" (Heb. 10:7).

One of the greatest prophetical types of the coming of Jesus as God's sacrificial Lamb is that of the passover lamb of Exodus, chapter 12. This lamb which was a type of Jesus must be a perfect lamb. "Your lamb shall be without blemish, a male of the first year: ye shall take it out from the sheep, or from the goats" (Exod. 12:5). It was to be scrutinized for any imperfection; it was to be absolutely perfect because it symbolized a perfect Saviour. The blood must be shed; it had to be applied by faith. Not a bone of it was to be broken and God said, "When I see the blood I will pass over you."

My friend, God requires blood for forgiveness. The best that natural man has to offer falls short of meeting the holy demands of an offended God. He requires the shedding and application of the blood. Jesus was the perfect fulfillment of the passover lamb. "The next day John seeth Jesus coming unto him, and saith, Behold the Lamb of God, which taketh away the sin of the world" (John 1:29).

In the Old Testament we see a great progression of truth concerning the lamb. In the lamb offered by Abel, we see a lamb for an individual. In the passover lamb, we see a lamb for a family. In the lamb of Leviticus offered on the day of atonement, we see a lamb for a nation. But in God's Lamb, the Lord Jesus Christ, we see a Lamb for the sins of the whole world. "Behold the Lamb of God which taketh away the sin of the world."

Yes, the sacrificial death of Jesus Christ was prophesied and God kept His word. Thank God that Jesus came into the world to die for sinners! He is God's remedy for sin; the only means of forgiveness and the only way to Heaven.

"The blood of Jesus Christ his Son cleanseth us from all sin."—I John 1:7.

III. The Sacrificial Death of Jesus Christ Means Eternal, Abundant Life to Us

The greatest truth ever uttered, the most sublime statement ever heard is that "Christ died for sinners." This is often expressed in the Word of God.

"Christ died for the ungodly."—Rom. 5:6.
"Christ died for us."—Rom. 5:8.
"Christ died for our sins according to the scriptures."—I Cor. 15:3.
"If one [Christ] died for all...."—II Cor. 5:14.

Now why did Christ die? Why was His death, His suffering, the shedding of His blood necessary? There is more than one scriptural answer to this question of the ages. He died to destroy the work of Satan, to offset the sin of Adam, to put away sin, to reveal the true nature of man, to reveal the true nature of God, and to satisfy His just and holy demands. Perhaps, though, the most glorious and wonderful purpose of His death is that we might have life. Without His glorious death on Calvary, our death spiritually and eternally would be eternal, unalterable. The sentence of death is upon all men. The Book of God leaves no doubt about this.

"All we like sheep have gone astray; we have turned every one to his own way; and the Lord hath laid on him the iniquity of us all."—Isa. 53:6.
"For the wages of sin is death; but the gift of God is eternal life through Jesus Christ our Lord."—Rom. 6:23.
"The soul that sinneth, it shall die."—Ezek. 18:4,20.

"For as in Adam all die, even so in Christ shall all be made alive."—I Cor. 15:22.

Christ's sacrificial death was to cancel the sentence of death upon all who believe on Him. Jesus said, "I am come that they might have life, and that they might have it more abundantly" (John 10:10). Now, He died that this abundant life might be expressed through us in three ways.

1. He died that we might live through Him. "In this was manifested the love of God toward us, because that God sent his only begotten Son into the world, that we might live through him" (I John 4:9).

Jesus expressed this great truth in John 12:24, "Verily, verily, I say unto you, Except a corn of wheat fall into the ground and die, it abideth alone: but if it die, it bringeth forth much fruit."

When I was a small boy I learned the lesson of life through death. I would dig down into the sand on the farm where I was raised to find the grains of corn to see why they hadn't come up. I would find that death and decay had set in, but out of the corrupting grain of corn had started a little green sprout of new life. Life through death!

2. He died that we might have life for Him. "For the love of Christ constraineth us; because we thus judge, that if one died for all, then were all dead: And that he died for all, that they which live should not henceforth live unto themselves, but unto him which died for them, and rose again" (II Cor. 5:14,15). Those for whom He died must not only enjoy life through Him but must live that life "for Him," as it is translated in the Amplified New Testament.

3. He died a sacrificial death, not only that we might have life through Him and for Him, but He died that we might have life with Him. "For God hath not appointed us to wrath, but to obtain salvation by our Lord Jesus Christ. Who died for us, that, whether we wake or sleep, we should live together with him" (I Thess. 5:9,10). Jesus wants the

redeemed with Him. He often expressed it; it seemed to be ever on His heart and only His death at Calvary could make this desire of Jesus a reality.

> *"Father, I will that they also, whom thou hast given me, be with me where I am; that they may behold my glory, which thou hast given me: for thou lovedst me before the foundation of the world."—John 17:24.*
> *"And if I go and prepare a place for you, I will come again, and receive you unto myself; that where I am, there ye may be also."—John 14:3.*

This desire of Jesus is shared by every true believer, the desire to be with Jesus. Paul expressed it more than once.

> *"For I am in a strait betwixt two, having a desire to depart, and to be with Christ; which is far better."—Phil. 1: 23.*
> *"We are confident, I say, and willing rather to be absent from the body, and to be present with the Lord."—II Cor. 5:8.*

What sweet and wonderful assurance as we look backward to the finished work of Calvary. We have life because He had death.

> *"The blood of Jesus Christ his Son cleanseth us from all sin."—I John 1:7.*

IV. The Blood of Christ Is God's Complete Answer to Sin

The problem of sin has no solution apart from the blood of the Lord Jesus Christ. In the Bible we read of three things we cannot do without.

> *"Without me ye can do nothing."—John 15:3.*
> *"Without faith it is impossible to please him."—Heb. 11:6.*
> *"Without shedding of blood is no remission."—Heb. 9:22.*

The wise philosopher of the ages has no answer to the sin problem. The modernist has no answer, the intellectual has no answer. Religion has no answer. Only God has the answer to man's sin and that is the cleansing blood of Jesus Christ.

No one has ever been saved apart from blood. Before Calvary people were saved by looking forward to the cross and the death of the Lamb. Now, men are saved by looking backward to the cross.

The preaching of the blood is a demonstration of the power of God. "For the preaching of the cross is to them that perish foolishness; but unto us which are saved it is the power of God" (I Cor. 1:18). The blood and the blood alone can bring peace to the human heart. "And, having made peace through the blood of his cross, by him to reconcile all things unto himself; by him, I say, whether they be things in earth, or things in heaven" (Col. 1:20).

The blood is the difference between the world and eternal life. It is the difference between life and death; the difference between freedom and slavery; the difference between a fiery judgment and eternal bliss. The blood of Jesus Christ is the difference between sin and salvation. The blood takes away sin, puts away sin, judges sin. "...but now once in the end of the world hath he appeared to put away sin by the sacrifice of himself" (Heb. 9:26b). The blood of Christ is God's way of separating the sinner from his sins. Notice what the Word of God tells us that God does with our sins.

1. He blots them out. "I have blotted out, as a thick cloud, thy transgressions, and, as a cloud, thy sins: return unto me; for I have redeemed thee" (Isa. 44:22).

2. He puts them in the depths of the ocean. "He will turn again, he will have compassion upon us; he will subdue our iniquities; and thou wilt cast all their sins into the depths of the sea" (Micah 7:19).

3. He removes them as far as the east is from the west. "As far as the east is from the west, so far hath he removed our transgressions from us" (Ps. 103:12).

4. He puts them behind His back. "For thou hast cast all my sins behind thy back" (Isa. 38:17).

In 1922 when the World's Fair met in Chicago, the World's Fair invited a representative from every major religion in the world. Men came from all over the world. There were Buddhists. There were representatives of Confucianism. There were the Mohammedan representatives. Catholic, Protestant, Jew, and Gentile, and every major religion in the world—all were represented.

It is said that they had a leader from every religion on earth sitting in a large conference room. It is said that one brought up a question and asked for an answer. He referred to Shakespeare's play, "Lady Macbeth," to the particular time when Lady Macbeth, who had committed murder and whose hands were stained red with the blood of the one she had killed, and whose soul and heart was stained with guilt before God, lifted up her bleeding hands and cried, 'Oh, damned spot, who can cleanse this blood away?'

One after another was asked, "Can your religion take that blood from the hands of Lady Macbeth? Can your religion make her clean, she who had murdered and stands with a guilty conscience and guilty heart before God?"

One man after another arose and said, "My religion cannot remove the stain, but had I known Lady Macbeth, and had I introduced her to our system of teaching, we could have kept her from committing the murder in the first place."

The leader of fundamentalism, the representative of Bible Christianity was Joe Cook, a godly man from Boston, Massachusetts. It is said that when they came to Joe Cook, he arose to his full height, and with a gleam in his eye and confidence in his face, he said, "I thank God I represent a religion that can take the bloody hands of Lady Macbeth and make them as clean as if they had never been stained with blood." And for some twenty minutes he preached the Gospel of cleansing power through the blood of Jesus.

Oh, thank God, men and women, this Bible does not just set forth a form of religion that will keep men good, but it sets forth a wonderful plan of blood atonement that will take a man who has never been good and who is stained with sin and guilty before God, and make him as clean as if he had never sinned, and justify him in God's sight and make him as white as the snow. No other Gospel, no other word has that power—the power of the Gospel of the blood atonement.

"The blood of Jesus Christ his Son cleanseth us from all sin."—I John 1:7.

V. The Blood of Jesus Is Precious to God and His Church

"Forasmuch as ye know that ye were not redeemed with corruptible things, as silver and gold, from your vain conversation received by tradition from your fathers; But with the precious blood of Christ, as of a lamb without blemish and without spot."—I Pet. 1:18, 19.

It is precious because of it cleansing from the past. It cleanses for the present and sets us free from sin's power. It gives us access to God.

The Devil has a great many subtle substitutes for true, scriptural salvation in Christ Jesus. Satan is perfectly satisfied when he can blindly lead folks to seek access to God in some way besides through the precious blood of Christ.

I think Satan's most damnable and most subtle plan is to get a sinner to seek a "feeling" or an experience instead of seeking Christ. God's plan of salvation is faith first, in the fact of His Word, and then comes feeling. Satan would have us reverse this order and have us seek a feeling, then faith.

Salvation is by faith, not by feeling! A man once said to me, "Yes, I want to be saved and I do believe but I don't have the feeling and 'they say' I should have feeling."

What "they say" is of little or no consequence. It is what God says that matters! "For by grace are ye saved through faith; and that not of yourselves: it is the gift of God" (Eph. 2:8). I am a minister of the Gospel. I have preached God's Word for thirty-three years. I know I am saved and I feel saved, but my assurance is not based on my feelings. The only reason I know I am saved is because God says so in His Word. May God help you to believe on Christ and be saved.

Another of the Devil's substitutes for salvation is morality or good works. We do not work to be saved at all. We are not baptized in order to be saved. Neither do we join the church in order that we might inherit eternal life. We are baptized and join the church because we are saved and not to be saved. Salvation is apart and distinct from all works, ordinances, creeds or organizations. "Not of works, lest any man should boast" (Eph. 2:9). If it were possible for us to obtain eternal life by our own good works, then Christ has died in vain and we do not need a Saviour but an example! Jesus and Jesus only can save from sin and Hell. "He that believeth on me hath everlasting life" (John 6:47).

Another of the Devil's substitutes for salvation is a passive belief in God. You may believe in the telephones and radios and yet never use them. Believing that there is a God will not save you. Believing that Jesus was born of a virgin, conceived by the Holy Spirit, and that He died at Calvary is one thing, but trusting that Christ as your Saviour is another. You must trust Him as your personal, individual Saviour. Demons believed and trembled but were not saved! To believe on Him is to commit yourself to Him. May God help you to take Christ now. "For the wages of sin is death; but the gift of God is eternal life through Jesus Christ our Lord" (Rom. 6:23).

A Southern Baptist preacher for whom I was conducting a revival meeting told me this story. Two young men were very devoted friends. In spite of the fact that one of the young men was the only son of a millionaire and the other the son of a poverty-stricken widow, the young men loved each other and were almost inseparable.

When America entered the World War of 1914, these two men enlisted together, one a pauper, the other wealthy. The two companions fought side by side throughout some of the great battles of the war. One night the rich young man was fatally wounded on the blood-soaked battlefields of France. His friend crawled through the mud and darkness and reached the wounded, dying boy and held him in his arms as he died. As the young man died, he looked into the face of his poor but loyal friend whom he loved and said, "Pal, I'm dying now. I am my father's only son. My father is rich. You are poor. I want you to take this shirt off my body. It is soaked with my own blood. If you live through this awful war and get back to the United States, take this bloody shirt to my father. Tell him how I died and tell him how I loved you. Tell him that it was my dying request that he adopt you as his own son and make you heir to all his riches."

A few months later found the poor young man back in America being ushered into the large library of a beautiful palatial residence in one of the large eastern cities, where he was soon to meet the father of his dead companion. The father entered the room and the young man told him the story and also the dying request of his son. "How do I know you are telling the truth?" the elderly man said. "How do I know but what this is a scheme for you to become heir to my wealth?"

In answer to this question the young soldier unwrapped the bloody shirt which bore the initials of the millionaire's son. When the father saw the bloody shirt he said, "I take you as my own son, and you shall be my own and I shall be your father and you shall be heir to all I have!"

That is just what God wants to do for you. You are a poor sinner, but through the merits of His precious shed blood, you can become a child of God and a joint heir with Jesus Christ. "When I see the blood I will pass over you."

Sinner, apply the blood of Christ to your heart now!

> When I survey the wondrous cross,
>   On which the Prince of Glory died;
> My richest gain I count but loss,
>   And pour contempt on all my pride.
>
> Were the whole realm of nature mine,
>   That were a present far too small;
> Love so amazing, so divine,
>   Demands my soul, my life, my all.

"The blood of Jesus Christ his Son cleanseth us from all sin."—I John 1:7.

VI. The Blood of Jesus Is Hated by Satan and Opposed by Modernism

Just as you see the trail of redemptive blood throughout the Bible, so you see the hatred of Satan against the precious blood throughout the Bible. Cain hated the blood of Abel's lamb and Pharaoh despised the blood of the passover lamb. Even Christians sometimes do not attach the importance to the blood that God attaches. This was true of Simon Peter. In almost the same breath in which he spoke so eloquently of the deity of Christ, he minimized the essentiality of the cross.

"From that time forth began Jesus to shew unto his disciples, how that he must go unto Jerusalem, and suffer many things of the elders and chief priests and scribes, and be killed, and be raised again the third day. Then Peter took him, and began to rebuke him, saying, Be it far from thee, Lord: this shall not be unto thee. But he turned, and said unto Peter, Get thee behind me, Satan: thou art an offence unto me: for thou savourest not the things that be of God, but those that be of men."—Matt. 16:21-23.

Peter thought there might be some easier way, some shortcut to salvation other than the blood and death of Jesus Christ. There is no other way out of bondage into freedom except by the blood of Christ. Satan spoke against the blood through Peter.

The dying thieves at the time of the crucifixion of Jesus thought there should be some way out except by the cross and by blood.

"Then were there two thieves crucified with him, one on the right hand, and another on the left. And they that passed by reviled him, wagging their heads, And saying, Thou that destroyest the temple, and buildest it in three days, save thyself. If thou be the Son of God, come down from the cross. Likewise also the chief priests mocking him, with the scribes and elders, said, He saved others; himself he cannot save. If he be the King of Israel, let him now come down from the cross, and we will believe him. He trusted in God; let him deliver him now, if he will have him: for he said, I am the Son of God. The thieves also, which were crucified with him, cast the same in his teeth."—Matt. 27: 38-44.

The cry of the thieves and even the lost but religious leaders was, "Come down from the cross." Apart from the cross there is no way to be saved.

Modernists hate the blood. Oftentimes denominational Sunday school literature either mocks at the blood or completely ignores it, and it is never mentioned in much of modern-day religious literature. I have heard of church after church which has eliminated all the songs in hymnals which have to do with the blood atonement, the crucifixion, Calvary or the death of Christ.

Yes, Satan hates the blood of Jesus Christ. But thank God for the blood; it is the sinner's hope and the Christian's safety and security.

"The blood of Jesus Christ his Son cleanseth us from all sin."—I John 1:7.

VII. The Blood of Jesus Christ Is the Theme of Heaven's Song

"Unto him that loved us, and washed us from our sins in his own blood."—Rev. 1:5b.

"And they sung a new song, saying, Thou art worthy to take the book, and to open the seals thereof: for thou wast slain, and hast redeemed us to God by thy blood out of every kindred, and tongue, and people, and nation."—Rev. 5:9.

"And they sing the song of Moses the servant of God, and the song of the Lamb, saying, Great and marvelous are thy works, Lord God Almighty; just and true are thy ways, thou King of saints."—Rev. 15:3.

Yes, the theme of the Bible is the song of Heaven. The saints of all ages in heavenly chorus shall forever extol the precious saving and cleansing blood of the Lord Jesus Christ. Let everything that hath breath praise God for the blood.

My friend, are you sure today that you have been washed in Jesus' blood? May I invite you to come to Calvary where God has opened an eternal fountain for sin and uncleanness.

"The blood of Jesus Christ his Son cleanseth us from all sin."—I John 1:7.

> E'er since by faith I saw the stream,
>   Thy flowing wounds supply,
> Redeeming love has been my theme,
>   And shall be till I die.
>
> Then in a nobler, sweeter song
>   I'll sing thy power to save,
> When this poor lisping, stamm'ring tongue
>   Lies silent in the grave.

THE RESURRECTION OF JESUS CHRIST

"He shewed himself alive after his passion [suffering] *by many infallible proofs, being seen of them forty days, and speaking of the things pertaining to the kingdom of God."*— *Acts 1:3.*

I. The Prophecy of the Resurrection

II. The Proof of the Resurrection

III. The Purpose of the Resurrection

IV. The Power of the Resurrection

V. The People of the Resurrection

VI. A Part of God's Saving Gospel

VII. The Physical Reality of the Resurrection

The Garden Tomb at the foot of Mount Calvary

"The angel answered, . . . Fear not ye: for I know that ye seek Jesus, which was crucified. He is not here: for he is risen, as he said. Come, see the place where the Lord lay." —Matt. 28:5, 6.

7

The Resurrection of Jesus Christ

"He shewed himself alive after his passion [suffering] *by many infallible proofs, being seen of them forty days, and speaking of the things pertaining to the kingdom of God."*— *Acts 1:3.*

I want you to see the importance of the resurrection of Jesus Christ. Satan hates this doctrine. He has always opposed it because it is a part of the Gospel and it makes Christianity superior to all other religions of the world. I don't care what your religion may be, whether it is the Moslem religion or the Buddhist religion or any religion you may consider, Christianity—if I may call it that in its correct sense, is the only religion that can point to an empty tomb where the blessed Saviour conquered death and arose from the grave. The resurrection of Jesus Christ makes Christianity superior to all other religions. It guarantees a judgment and assures Satan's defeat. I do not know of any doctrine that Satan hates any more than He does the doctrine of the resurrection of Jesus Christ.

You remember in Jesus' day and in Paul's day, there were those who said there could not possibly be any such thing as a resurrection. There was a great group of people called the Sadducees, along with the Pharisees, who were prominent in Jesus' day.

Now the Sadducees were a group of people who did not believe in any kind of miracle. They were religious people but they said, "Miracles are out of the question. You can rationalize and explain anything. There is no such thing as a miracle." Now in order to be consistent with that belief, they had to say there was no such thing as the resurrection.

In Matthew 22:23 we read, "The same day came to him the Sadducees, which say that there is no resurrection...." So, in Jesus' day, before He even died on the cross, there were people who said there is no such thing as a resurrection.

Now Paul faced this same unbelief. In First Corinthians, chapter 15, which is the greatest chapter in the Bible on the subject of the resurrection, Paul wrote to the church at Corinth, and said, "...how say some among you that there is no resurrection of the dead?" (vs. 12). So even in the city of Corinth where for eighteen months Paul had preached the blessed Word of God, there were people who said there was no resurrection of the dead.

Down through the years Satan has tried to get people to believe there is no such thing as the resurrection of Jesus Christ. In Acts 26:8 Paul said, "Why should it be thought a thing incredible with you, that God should raise the dead?" This matter of the resurrection has always been hated by the Devil; taught in the Word of God but despised by the enemy of truth.

It is said that some years ago there were two brilliant young men in England, one named Lyttelton and the other named West. These two young men, both unbelievers, got together and said, "If we could disprove two great things that Christians believe the Bible teaches, we could knock the foundation from under so-called Christian truth." They said, "If we could disprove that Paul was ever converted on the Damascus Road..." (and there is a reason for this because in that conversion Paul heard the audible voice of Jesus Christ who had been crucified; he heard Him speak from Heaven; and he saw the light of His divine glory shine upon him). They said, "We must disprove the conversion of the Apostle Paul on the road to Damascus."

Another truth they wanted to disprove was the resurrection of Jesus Christ from the grave. So these two brilliant young men said to each other, "I will take one subject; you take the other. We will spend twelve months of arduous study and laborious research. We will come together at the end of the year and study our findings."

So for twelve months one studied the conversion of the Apostle Paul and the other, the resurrection of Jesus Christ. At the end of the year, they met. One said, "I have come to know that it is an actual fact that Saul of Tarsus was converted on the Damascus road. It is an historical truth and a Bible truth. And in studying it I, too, have come to know Jesus Christ as my personal Saviour."

The other young man said, "I have studied the resurrection and as I have studied it, I have found it to be not only a biblical truth but an historical fact that on the third day Jesus conquered death and triumphantly walked out of the tomb. I, too, have been saved."

Those two men, who set out to disprove the resurrection of Jesus and His saving work, were both gloriously saved and became great witnesses for Jesus Christ.

I am saying this to you because I want you to see the importance of the resurrection. You find in the Bible this suggestion: Suppose Jesus had not risen from the grave. Then what would be the result of no resurrection? Suppose Jesus had been the Son of God. Suppose He had been born of a virgin. Suppose He had died on the cross, robed in blood and crowned with thorns. But suppose He had not walked out of the tomb. Suppose there had been no resurrection!

Paul brings this up in the fifteenth chapter of First Corinthians, "But if there be no resurrection of the dead, then is Christ not risen: If there be no such thing as the resurrection, then Jesus Christ was conquered by death. His body decayed in the tomb, if there be no such thing as the resurrection."

In the second place, Paul said, "And if Christ be not risen, then is our preaching vain, and your faith is also vain. Yea, and we are found false witnesses of God; because we have testified of God that he raised up Christ: whom he raised not up, if so be that the dead rise not" (vss. 14,15). Paul said, 'If there is no resurrection, we are false witnesses. If there is no resurrection, we are the greatest group of liars the world has ever known.'

He said, "And if Christ be not raised, your faith is vain; ye are yet in your sins" (vs. 17). Paul said, 'You are not even saved; you are yet in your sins, if there is no resurrection of the dead.'

He said, 'If there be no resurrection, then the dead have perished. You will never see your loved ones again. They have gone back to dust. There is no life beyond the grave. There is no future hope. There is no place called Heaven. Your dead are perished.'

In the seventh place, he said, "If in this life only we have hope in Christ, we are of all men most miserable" (vs. 19). He said, 'If there is no resurrection from the grave, we are the most pitiful group of people that ever lived.'

Now, when you contemplate this, you are bound to say with me, "There is nothing in this world more important than the resurrection of Jesus Christ."

Someone has said that the resurrection of Jesus Christ is called the keystone of all Bible truth. If you were to visit the Holy Land and European countries, as it has been my privilege to do, you would see many, many arches. You would see the Arch of Triumph in Paris, the Arch of Titus at Rome, and many others. Those arches are built of stone; they are not supported by steel. And they have stood through many centuries and have not fallen, for people knew how to build arches. In an arch there is one stone that is more important than any other, and that is called the keystone. It is a large V-shaped stone that stands right in the middle of the top of the arch, and all the weight of other stones rests upon it. The arch does not fall as long as the keystone remains secure.

I am saying to you this morning, the keystone of all the truth by which you have been saved, or all the truth in which you believe, the foundation of all your life, according to the

Bible, is the resurrection of Jesus Christ out of the grave. It is the most important doctrine taught in the Bible.

There is so much about the resurrection! Ten actual resurrections are recorded in the Bible, three in the Old Testament and seven in the New Testament, and these do not include the future resurrections and events yet to come relating to Jesus Christ. The resurrection of Jesus is mentioned forty times in the New Testament. Forty times God takes up the subject, in passages of Scripture that discuss the resurrection.

The preaching of the early church was based on the resurrection of Christ. Again and again and again you find it emphasized. When they elected one to take the place of Judas Iscariot, they said, "We want to elect one to be a witness of the fact that Jesus Christ arose from the dead." The resurrection was the central theme of all their preaching, talking, fellowshiping, and witnessing in Bible days, and in the book of Acts. There is nothing more important than the resurrection of Jesus Christ.

Now I would like to discuss seven things about the resurrection of Jesus Christ from the grave.

I. The Prophecy of the Resurrection

First of all I want you to see the prophecy of the resurrection. This is not just something that happened and people had no way of knowing that it was going to happen. The resurrection of Jesus Christ was predicted and prophesied just like many other things in the Bible had been.

For instance, when they came to Jesus and said, "Show us a sign from Heaven that you are the Son of God," Jesus said, "There shall no sign be given you as to who I am and what I mean to do except of the prophet Jonah." Then Jesus said, "For as Jonas was three days and three nights in the whale's belly; so shall the Son of man be three days and three nights in the heart of the earth" (Matt. 12:40). Jesus Christ, long before He ever died, said, "Just as Jonah was in the belly of the fish three days and three nights and came out alive, so shall the Son of God be in the heart of the earth and come forth again." Jesus Himself said, "I am going to rise from the grave."

We read in Matthew, chapter 16, that He called His twelve disciples together and told them that "he must go unto Jerusalem, and suffer many things of the elders and chief priests and scribes, and be killed, and be raised again the third day" (vs. 21). Now let me tell you something: just as sure as Jesus died on that cross, just so sure it is that He came out of that tomb of Joseph of Arimathea alive! And He predicted His resurrection.

We find in the second chapter of the Gospel of John, verses 19 and 21, one of the greatest statements Jesus ever made. He said, "Destroy this temple, and in three days I will raise it up...." They didn't know what He was talking about. They said, "Forty and six years was this temple in building, and wilt thou rear it up in three days?" (vs. 20). Jesus said, 'I am not talking about that. You destroy this body, put it on a cross, put a spear in the side, a crown of thorns upon the brow, nails in the hands and feet, let Me hang those hours of feverish pain upon the cross, and let Me die; destroy this body if you will, but on the third day I am going to rebuild it again.' Thank God, He did!

In John 10:17,18 Jesus said, "I lay down my life, that I might take it again. No man taketh it from me, but I lay it down of myself. I have power to lay it down [that is, to die on the cross of Calvary] and I have power to take it again [that is, to rise again the third day]." So the resurrection of Jesus Christ was prophesied, first of all, by Jesus Himself and, secondly, it was predicted by typology in the Bible.

You can go back through the Old Testament and find pictures of the resurrection.

I am not guessing; I am telling you that Abraham believed in the resurrection of Jesus Christ. You read in the book of Genesis, chapter 22, of the offering of Isaac. Isaac, beyond any shadow of doubt, is a type of Jesus Christ. In verse 6 we see Isaac with the wood on his back. That is a type of the cross. "And they came to the place which God had told him of; and Abraham built an altar there, and laid the wood in order, and bound Isaac his son, and laid him on the altar upon the wood" (vs. 9). Mount Moriah where Abraham built the altar, is an extension of Mount Calvary, so they were literally on the same mountain where Jesus was to die. "Abraham...saw the place afar off. And Abraham said unto his young men, Abide ye here with the ass; and I and the lad will go yonder and worship, and come again to you" (Gen. 22:5). He said, 'We are going to worship, and we are coming back.' He went up on top of that mountain, bound Isaac's hands behind him—a type of Jesus—laid him on an altar, and reached in his clothing and took the sacrificial knife and standing on that mountain, anticipating the death and resurrection of Jesus, Abraham lifted that knife above the body of his son; then, all at once, an unseen hand stayed his hand. A voice said, "Abraham, over in the thicket is a ram caught by the horns. It is a substitute. Put that on the altar and let it be slain; Isaac must be raised." Thank God, down from the mountainside came Abraham and Isaac.

Why do I know that is a type of the resurrection of Jesus? Looking back through Calvary and back through an empty tomb, Hebrews 11:17-19 says, "By faith Abraham, when he was tried, offered up Isaac: and he that had received the promises offered up his only begotten son. Of whom it was said, That in Isaac shall thy seed be called: Accounting that God was able to raise him up, even from the dead; from whence also he received him in a figure." Jesus said, "Your father Abraham rejoiced to see my day: and he saw it and was glad" (John 8:56). Abraham believed that God was able to raise up Isaac because he believed in the resurrection of Jesus Christ. So the resurrection of Jesus is set forth in the Bible by type.

I see in Joseph a type of Jesus and His resurrection.

Placed down in a pit; his coat made bloody and showed to his father, who gave him up as dead; sold and betrayed by his own brethren, Joseph went into bondage, rose to power, and redeemed the lives of his brothers when they were doomed to death by famine. Then Joseph was restored alive to his father. I see in this a type of the resurrection of Jesus Christ.

Suppose you lived when Jesus lived. Three times He raised the dead. One time He raised a little twelve-year-old girl. One time He raised a young man of maybe twenty or twenty-one years of age. Then he raised a man who had probably lived most of his normal life. Someone has said that Jesus raised the dead, the deader and the deadest. He raised a twelve-year-old girl whose body was still warm, a young man who had been dead just long enough that his mother was on the way out of the city to bury him, and a man who had already been in the tomb four days. Of the last one, Lazarus, his sister Martha said, "Lord, by this time he stinketh: for he hath been dead four days." Jesus raised the dead, the deader, and the deadest.

Suppose you had been alive during the ministry of Jesus and you had seen Him raise the twelve-year-old girl. You would have heard the parents say, "My daughter died. He brought her back to life!"

Suppose you could have heard that mother in the city of Nain, that little city nestled at the foot of a mountain—suppose you could have heard her say, "My husband died, then my son died, and I had no one left. I was on my way to the cemetery when I met Jesus, and He raised my boy!"

Suppose you could have heard Mary and Martha and Lazarus praising the Lord. "Jesus raised our loved one!" the women would have said. If I had heard that, I would have said, "Now if He can raise a girl, a young man, and a man who had been locked in the tomb four days, there is not one shadow of doubt in my mind that if He says He is coming out of a tomb, He is coming out!" Thank God, He did! There are types of the resurrection of Jesus Christ.

I see the resurrection foretold even in the record of the crucifixion of Christ. You know, mysterious, wonderful things happened at Calvary. But they assure us of not only a finished work of atonement but a completed work of salvation in the resurrection. For instance, in Matthew 27 we read of four miraculous things that took place when Jesus died.

First of all, there was an earthquake. Secondly, the veil of the Temple was rent from the top to the bottom, not from the bottom to the top but from the top to the bottom; salvation came *down* from God. The veil was rent asunder and there for the first time is the holy of holies with the sprinkled blood completely exposed so that anyone can see the atoning blood.

In the third place, there was a phenomenal darkness. For three hours God pushed the sun back into oblivion, and darkness came at noonday.

In the fourth place, I read in Matthew 27:52, "And the graves were opened; and many bodies of the saints which slept arose." Think of it! While Jesus is hanging on the cross graves are opening and Christian people who had died got up out of the graves after the resurrection and went into the city. So even while there was the dripping of the blood and the dying of God's Lamb, graves were being opened.

I see it again in the words of one of the thieves. He said to Jesus, "Lord, remember me when thou comest into thy kingdom" (Luke 23:42). Jesus, with a crown of thorns, robed in blood, suspended between Heaven and earth on a cross, and dying, said to him, "To day shalt thou be with me in paradise." Even the dying thief said, in effect: "That's not the end of Him. He is coming off that cross, He will walk through that tomb, He will put a light of immortality in it. There is a kingdom of God yet to come, and I want to be in it." The thief said, "Remember me! Re-

member me!" Jesus said, 'All right. I am going to have a
kingdom and I am going to remember you.' This Jesus could
not have said unless He was going to rise from the dead.

The prophecy of the resurrection!

*"He shewed himself alive after his passion by many in-
fallible proofs...."—Acts 1:3.*

II. The Proof of the Resurrection

I want you to notice with me the proof of the resurrection.
Our text says, "He shewed himself alive after his passion
[suffering] by many infallible proofs." You say to me, "How
do you know Jesus Christ arose from the dead? How can
you prove that?" Well, I can prove it; if I couldn't, I would
quit preaching. If I didn't believe it deep down in my heart,
with an absorbing, life-changing conviction, I would never
preach again.

I believe it, first of all, because the Word of God teaches
it—the Word of God which has proved itself to me. In Luke
24:4 you read that when the women from Galilee came to the
tomb of Jesus to anoint His body with spices and ointments,
"two men [angels] stood by them in shining garments."
Some disciples came to the tomb very early that first
Lord's Day morning. And there was the empty tomb! Just
forty days later they would see Him go up into Heaven and
two men in shining garments standing by. So on the resurrection morning the disciples go to the tomb and here are
two men again standing at the empty tomb and they say to
them, "He is not here; but is risen" (Luke 24:6). The Bible
thus announces that Jesus Christ arose from the dead.

Let me say this to you: He who denies the resurrection
of Christ, denies the inspiration of the blessed Holy Bible,
for the Word of God teaches the truth of the resurrection.

First Corinthians 15:20 says, "But now is Christ risen
from the dead, and become the firstfruits of them that
slept."

Romans 4:25 states that Christ was "delivered for our

offences, and was raised again for our justification."

The Bible declares more than forty times in the New Testament alone that Jesus Christ arose from the dead.

You say, "Do you have other proof?" Yes, I do. I believe that Jesus Christ rose from the dead because of the presence and work of the Holy Spirit in my life and in yours. In John 14:16,17 is recorded the wonderful promise of Jesus about what would happen after He died and arose from the grave: "And I will pray the Father, and he shall give you another Comforter, that he may abide with you for ever; Even the Spirit of truth; whom the world cannot receive, because it seeth him not, neither knoweth him: but ye know him; for he dwelleth with you, and shall be in you." He said, 'I am going to leave but I am going to send the Holy Spirit to be your Comforter.'

When I know in my life the glorious, holy Presence, the life-transforming Presence, the constantly-abiding Presence of the Holy Spirit of God, who walked across the threshold of my soul and life and has lived within me for all these thirty-some-odd years, that is proof to me that He who said, 'I am going to the tomb and back to Glory and am sending to you the Holy Spirit,' did just exactly what He said He would do.

In John 16:7-11 we read again of Jesus' promise to send the Holy Spirit:

"Nevertheless I tell you the truth; It is expedient for you that I go away: for if I go not away, the Comforter will not come unto you; but if I depart, I will send him unto you. And when he is come, he will reprove the world of sin, and of righteousness, and of judgment: Of sin, because they believe not on me; Of righteousness, because I go to my Father, and ye see me no more; Of judgment, because the prince of this world is judged."

Jesus said, 'When the Holy Spirit comes, after I rise from the dead and go to be with My Father, He will guide you.' Thank God, I have been guided by Him! Jesus said, 'He will teach you.' Thank God, I have been taught by Him! Jesus said, 'He will convict you.' Thank God, I have been convicted by Him! Jesus said, 'He will endue and empower you.' Thank God, I have known a measure of that! I know that Jesus arose because of the presence of the Holy Spirit.

Now think for a moment. Many Bible students have said that one of the great proofs of the resurrection of Jesus is the miraculous change that took place in believers after He arose from the dead. As an example, there was Simon Peter. Simon Peter failed the Lord Jesus. Simon Peter was not like Judas, who was never saved. He was a Christian, a born-again man of God. But Simon Peter followed afar off and warmed his hands at the Devil's fire, and finally did something almost unbelievable that a Christian would do. When he was asked, 'Are you one of His?' Simon Peter replied, "I am not." Again, when someone that stood by said his speech betrayed him, Peter began to "curse and to swear, saying, I know not the man" (Matt. 26:74). When he was accused of being one of the disciples of Jesus, Simon Peter said, "I don't belong to Him."

Peter was not even with the Lord in the hour of His trial, in the hour of his death.

The Lord rises from the grave, meets Peter and others at the Sea of Galilee; and one day when the Spirit of God comes, Simon Peter, a changed man, arises in the midst of the group and begins to preach and three thousand are saved! What caused the change in this man? What is the difference? The power of the resurrected Christ!

I know He arose because of the miraculous change in the lives of Christians. The power of the resurrected Christ!

There are two other reasons that I know Christ arose from the grave. One is the scientific and archeological analyses of the tomb. It has been my wonderful privilege a number of times to visit the tomb of Jesus. There is no greater experience that could ever come to a human being, outside of being saved, than to visit that empty tomb where

His blessed body was laid and where two angels stood, and from the Bible read the blessed story of the resurrection. I have had that privilege a good many times. It is a beautiful place, a garden, actually. The garden is near Calvary, where Jesus was crucified. I sat in that tomb and read the Scripture and thought of something I read years ago.

The city of Jerusalem has been destroyed by war more than any other city on the face of the earth. It has been destroyed so many times that its present elevation is approximately twenty feet higher than it was when Jesus walked through its streets. The tomb near Calvary and the garden were buried with debris and dirt for many, many years. The Bible says that this tomb of Joseph of Arimathaea was a new tomb wherein man never lay. So no one had ever been placed in that tomb; Jesus was the first.

When excavation was done and the tomb was discovered about a hundred years ago, and the complete excavation finished by General Gordon, they took part of the dirt from the tomb. The weight of all of it, and the heavy stones, had caved in one wall and dirt had filled the tomb. They have repaired it now. Scientists took this dirt out of the tomb, even scraped the stone, and subjected it to a careful chemical analysis, and they said, "No human body has ever decayed in this place. No body has ever decayed in this tomb." So by archeological proof I know Jesus Christ arose from the dead, and I know there is no evidence to the contrary.

The man who started the "House of David," Benjamin Pernell, is from right here in the State of Michigan, from Benton Harbor. He said that after he had been dead, the third day he would rise again. But he is still buried over there somewhere. Thank God, Jesus isn't! He arose from the grave; He is at the throne of grace this morning and He reaches out a hand to every sinner. The Bible says that if you believe in your heart that God raised Christ from the dead, "thou shalt be saved" (Rom. 10:9).

"He shewed himself alive after his passion by many infallible proofs...."—Acts 1:3.

III. The Purpose of the Resurrection

The Bible makes plain and clear the purpose of the resurrection of Jesus Christ. Why was it necessary that Jesus conquer death, that He arise from the grave, that He walk out of the tomb? Why was it necessary that Jesus arise from the grave?

First, to prove His deity. The proof of the deity of Jesus Christ depends upon this. He had promised that He would prove that He was the Son of God by His resurrection from the dead. When the scribes and Pharisees asked Him to give them a sign from Heaven to show who He was, that He was the Son of God, He answered, "An evil and adulterous generation seeketh after a sign; and there shall no sign be given to it, but the sign of the prophet Jonas: For as Jonas was three days and three nights in the whale's belly; so shall the Son of man be three days and three nights in the heart of the earth" (Matt. 12:39,40). Jesus said, 'The proof of my deity will be the fact that after I am crucified on the cross and have been three days in the bonds of death, I will come forth out of the tomb.'

Romans 1:4 says that Jesus Christ was "declared to be the Son of God with power, according to the spirit of holiness, by the resurrection from the dead." God's Word says that the resurrection of Jesus Christ declares Him to be the Son of God with power. The purpose of the resurrection is to prove His deity.

In the second place, the purpose of the resurrection is to assure our justification. There is a truth in the Bible that makes people feel secure in the Lord and makes them know that they are saved. That is what we call justification. I have often made a difference between regeneration and justification. Regeneration takes place in the heart. Regeneration is when Christ comes in and you are born the second time. God then imparts to you a new nature, a divine nature. Justification is something else.

Justification does not take place within you. It takes place in the mind of God. Justification, my friends, means that God declares you are a Christian, just as righteous as if you had never sinned. It is an act of God—the will of God. It is the sovereign purpose of God to declare you as righteous as if you had never sinned. That is justification.

Romans 4:25 says that Jesus "was delivered [to be crucified] for our offences, and was raised again for our justification," that is, to keep us saved eternally and keep us as clean in our standing before God as if we had never sinned. He was "delivered for our offences, and was raised again for our justification."

Romans 5:1 says, "Therefore being justified by faith, we have peace with God through our Lord Jesus Christ."

The purpose of the resurrection is, first of all, to prove His deity; secondly, to assure our justification; and, in the third place, to authenticate His redemption.

Just think; if Jesus had not arisen from the dead, no one would have believed that His work on the cross had any power in it whatsoever. This is a part of the Gospel. When Paul wrote his first epistle to the Corinthian church, he defined what the Gospel is: "...that Christ died for our sins according to the scriptures; And that he was buried, and that he rose again the third day according to the scriptures" (I Cor. 15:3,4). You would not have a completed Gospel were it not for the resurrection of the Lord Jesus Christ. The purpose of the resurrection is to authenticate Christ's redemption of sinful mankind.

In the fourth place, the purpose of the resurrection is to assure our own resurrection. So many in recent days have departed out of this life and out of this great church family of Emmanuel Baptist Church! A number of men who have been members of this church for a good many years have died recently. I never think of the homegoing of a saint of God but what my mind takes me to the Gospel of John, chapter 11, which tells of the death of Lazarus and of his sisters sending for Jesus before his death, with the hope that Jesus would heal their brother and raise him up. Brokenhearted, sorrowing Martha went to meet Jesus on the little road leading into Bethany, and when she saw Him she said, "Lord, if thou hadst been here, my brother had not died." Jesus said to her, "Thy brother shall rise again.... I am the resurrection, and the life: he that believeth in me, though he were dead, yet shall he live: And whosoever liveth and believeth in me shall never die. Believest thou this?"

Thank God, through the resurrection of Christ, I am guaranteed that I also shall be raised from the grave, unless the rapture takes place before my death. That is my hope. The coming of Christ and the resurrection of saved people is the hope of a Christian.

I want to bring you a solemn truth. You say, "What is the purpose of the resurrection of Jesus Christ?" It is to guarantee a judgment day. The resurrection, strange as it may sound, guarantees that men and women are going to stand before God at the judgment.

I read a sermon that Paul preached in the city of Athens in Greece. It has been our privilege a good many times to go up on that little rocky, stone mountain called Mars' Hill in Athens and read that sermon in the seventeenth chapter of the book of Acts, at the place where Paul stood when he preached it. In that sermon Paul said, "...God...now commandeth all men every where to repent: Because he hath appointed a day, in the which he will judge the world in righteousness by that man [Jesus] whom he hath ordained; whereof he hath given assurance unto all men, in that he hath raised him from the dead" (Acts 17:30,31).

Paul said that God has set aside a time in which he will judge the world. I say to you, my friends, that there is one thing wrong with the people of this world—they do not plan on ever being judged. One thing wrong with this world is that there is no fear of God in the hearts and minds of people. What is wrong with America, basically, fundamentally, is that there is no fear of God in this country any more.

We read that in this day and time no convict likes to be locked up, confined in a prison; but an actual study shows that convicts do not carry in their hearts a fear of confinement in prison. The study does show that a man who is a lawbreaker has a fear of that word "gallows" or the electric chair. What we need in this world today (and some of you will criticize this preacher for saying this) is some public hangings. You say, "Why, that is the cruelest thing I have ever heard!" No, that would be a merciful thing to do. If we had more hangings in public, where people could see them, we would have less violence and murder in our land. Do you know that in one year in this country several hundred people were killed with hand guns, while England had only thirty such killings, and France less than that. We are the most barbaric nation on the face of the earth. Why? Because there is no fear of God and no expectancy of judgment.

I come to read of the glorious resurrection of Jesus Christ from the grave and His entrance into glorious life. This Bible tells me that God has guaranteed a judgment day. I look back and say I know that Jesus arose, and I look forward and say I know there will be an hour of judgment, for the same Bible that tells us that He arose from the dead says that this is God's assurance unto all men that He is going to have a day of judgment.

If we can get people to fear God, we can get people to do right. I used to hear a story told of a soldier during the Civil War, standing around a fire, the night before a fierce battle expected the next day. The young man's face looked white and ashen in the light of the fire. An old veteran said to him, "What's wrong? Are you afraid to die?"

The young man said, "No, I am not afraid to die."

"Then," said the veteran, "why do you tremble? Why are you so quiet?"

"I am not afraid of death. I am afraid of what comes after death."

That is what Hebrews 9:27 says: "...it is appointed unto men once to die, but after this the judgment." The resurrection of Jesus Christ guarantees that God has already set a judgment day in which all men must stand before Him. The purpose of the resurrection is, among other things, that we may be guaranteed a judgment day, for this Bible says that every knee shall bow and every tongue confess "that Jesus Christ is Lord, to the glory of God the Father" (Phil. 2:11).

"He shewed himself alive after his passion by many infallible proofs...."—Acts 1:3.

IV. The Power of the Resurrection

I want you to notice the power of the resurrection of Jesus Christ. I have already quoted Romans 1:4, "And declared to be the Son of God with power, according to the spirit of holiness, by the resurrection from the dead."

The fifteenth chapter of I Corinthians has five great systems or sets of truth on the subject of immortality, life beyond the grave, resurrection out of the earth, etc. It is the great resurrection chapter of the Bible. In I Corinthians 15:43, a verse dealing with the resurrected body, we read: "...it is raised in power." More than once in the Bible we find that the word "power" is linked to the resurrection of Jesus Christ.

Philippians 3:10, where Paul is expressing great aspirations of his innermost heart and soul, reads: "That I may know him, and the power of his resurrection, and the fellowship of his sufferings, being made conformable unto his death." Paul said, 'My prayer is that I may know Christ in the power of His resurrection.'

One day some Sadducees came to Jesus, as people do in

this day and time, with a question that really was not important for their salvation or their eternal destiny or peace of mind. I do not know whether it was an actual case or a theoretical one, but they said:

"Master, Moses said, If a man die, having no children, his brother shall marry his wife, and raise up seed unto his brother. Now there were with us seven brethren: and the first, when he had married a wife, deceased, and having no issue, left his wife unto his brother: Likewise the second also, and the third, unto the seventh. And last of all the woman died also. Therefore in the resurrection whose wife shall she be of the seven? for they all had her."—Matt. 22: 24-28.

Jesus answered them: "Ye do err, not knowing the scriptures, nor the power of God" (vs. 29).

Now there is a power here—I want you to see it—a miraculous, divine power. Three days Jesus Christ was in a tomb with a Roman seal upon it and with a guard placed outside to see that no one came and stole the body. The Roman government said, "This tomb is sealed forever." Then the third day a white light shone from Heaven and the soldiers fell back as dead men and the stone rolled away and the door opened and there came walking out of the grave the blessed Son of God. The napkin that had bound His head to keep his mouth closed was lying folded. The graveclothes had been unwound and neatly laid aside. The resurrection, ordained and planned in the councils of God before He ever hung a star or made the heavens, took place, and Jesus walked out of the tomb alive! Talking about the power of God, there never has been and there never will be a greater demonstration of the miraculous power than Jesus' walking out of the grave. My friends, that is the power that is spoken of in connection with the resurrection that Paul meant when he wrote, "That I may know him, and the power of his resurrection..." (Phil. 3:10).

I believe that I can show you that the Bible teaches Christians should have a power like the manifest power of God in their lives. Ephesians 3:20 has always been a challenge to me. "Now unto him that is able to do exceeding abundantly above all that we ask or think, according to the power that worketh in us." What is that power? It is the power of the living Lord. It is the resurrection power. It is power over the world, over the flesh, and over the Devil. Thank God for the resurrection of Jesus Christ!

One of the sweetest stories I have ever heard—and it is a true story—is of a man by the name of Frederick Douglas, a colored man of a generation or two ago, who worked for freedom of the slaves. Frederick Douglas had suffered pressures, loss of freedom, and discouragement, but he was a Christian. It is said that one day, when he was scheduled to speak in Atlanta, Georgia, a great group of people had gathered to hear him. When he stood up to speak, he lost his composure and instead of beginning his address, he laid his hands on the pulpit, put his head on his hands, and began to weep. It is said that an old colored woman out in the audience took out a white handkerchief and waved it to get his attention. After a while, he looked up, saw her handkerchief, and heard her calling to him. He looked at her and she at him, and she said, "Mr. Douglas, I want to ask you a question today."

"What is it, ma'am?"

"Mr. Douglas, am God dead? Am God dead?"

He lifted his head higher and said, "No, Christ is very much alive."

That little old colored woman waved that white handkerchief and said, "Then, Mr. Douglas, if Jesus Christ is still living, no Christian should ever hang his head in defeat!"

I say to you, if Christ arose from the dead, and lives at the throne of Glory, then no Christian should ever live a life of defeat. Thank God, that power, the resurrection power, is available to all who seek and want it in their lives—the power to live the life sublime, the life that is above mediocrity, the life with God, the Christian life. That power, the resurrection power, is available to you.

"He shewed himself alive after his passion by many infallible proofs...."—Acts 1:3.

V. The People of the Resurrection

The fifth point of this subject is the people of the resurrection. In John, chapter 5, we read a great statement that Jesus gave concerning the resurrection of the dead. This needs to be clarified and thoroughly understood. Verses 28 and 29 of John, chapter 5, read:

"Marvel not at this: for the hour is coming, in the which all that are in the graves shall hear his voice, And shall come forth; they that have done good, unto the resurrection of life; and they that have done evil, unto the resurrection of damnation."

Notice here that there are two resurrections and two classes of people mentioned in one verse: "they that have done good, unto the resurrection of life; and they that have done evil, unto the resurrection of damnation."

When I was first saved and began to preach, I would read this verse and think of what might be called a general resurrection, and that was a mistake. I thought that both the saved and the lost would be raised out of the grave in the same day, that the saved would be with the Lord and the lost would be condemned to an eternal Hell forever. But there is no such thing as a general resurrection taught in the Bible. So I want you to see clearly the picture of the people of the resurrection.

First of all, the saved will be raised when Jesus comes again. By His coming again in this instance I mean what is called the rapture of the church, that is, the first part of His second coming, when He comes to receive the church unto Himself.

In I Thessalonians 4:13-17 is a wonderful passage that deals with the rapture of the church. Paul said:

"But I would not have you to be ignorant, brethren, concerning them which are asleep, that ye sorrow not, even as others which have no hope. For if we believe that Jesus died and rose again, even so them also which sleep in Jesus will God bring with him. For this we say unto you by the word of the Lord, that we which are alive and remain unto the coming of the Lord shall not prevent them which are asleep. For the Lord himself shall descend from heaven with a shout, with the voice of the archangel, and with the trump of God: and the dead in Christ shall rise first: Then we which are alive and remain shall be caught up together with them in the clouds, to meet the Lord in the air: and so shall we ever be with the Lord."

Notice first the statement: "the dead in Christ shall rise first." This is called the first resurrection, and it will take place at the time of the rapture of the church. This is talking about saved people when Jesus comes. From every cemetery across the face of the earth, from the bottom of the sea, from the tops of the mountains, from every battlefield, from every little silent City of the Dead where loved ones have been buried by their weeping families, Jesus shall raise every single one who sleeps in Jesus Christ.

But what about unsaved people? When will they be raised and brought out of the graves? When will their resurrection take place? You read in Revelation 20:5 this great statement: "But the rest of the dead lived not again until the thousand years were finished. This is the first resurrection." So you see the rest of the dead, the unsaved, lived not again until the thousand years have passed. Now actually and technically there will be one thousand *and seven years* between the resurrection of the saved and the resurrection of the lost. The resurrection of the saved will take place at the rapture. The resurrection of the lost will take place after the tribulation period and at the end of the millennial reign of our Lord and Saviour Jesus Christ. So there is no such thing taught in the Bible as a general resurrection. We read in Revelation 20:6, "Blessed and holy is he that hath part in the first resurrection: on such the second death hath no power...."

Now in this twentieth chapter of Revelation we learn that the unsaved dead are raised to stand before God in judgment, for we read, "And I saw the dead, small and great, stand before God; and the books were opened: and another book was opened, which is the book of life: and the dead were judged out of those things which were written in the books according to their words.... And whosoever was not found written in the book of life was cast into the lake of fire" (Rev. 20:12,15).

So you see the resurrection of the unsaved at the end of the millennial reign of Jesus on earth and then the great white throne judgment and then the second death, which is the lake of fire, which is eternal Hell for all those who do not believe in the Son of God as their personal Saviour. So we have in the Bible the clear teaching about the people of the resurrection.

"He shewed himself alive after his passion by many infallible proofs...."—Acts 1:3.

VI. A Part of God's Saving Gospel

Then in the sixth place, the resurrection is a part of God's saving Gospel. A good many times lately, in dealing with what I might call the doctrines of Christ, or the doctrines that relate to the Lord Jesus Christ, I have defined out of the Word of God what we call the Gospel of God's grace, the Gospel that is preached to the salvation of souls —and that definition is found in I Corinthians 15:3 and 4 where Paul says, "...I delivered unto you first of all that which I also received, how that Christ died for our sins according to the scriptures; And that he was buried, and that he rose again the third day according to the scriptures." So the resurrection of Jesus Christ is a part, a vital part, a life-giving part of God's saving Gospel.

You will see this in a number of places. For instance, Paul wrote in Romans 10:8 and 9 that "the word of faith, which we preach," or the Gospel, is "That if thou shalt confess with thy mouth the Lord Jesus, and shalt believe in thine heart that God hath raised him from the dead, thou shalt be saved." You say to me, "Preacher, do you mean to say that you have to believe in the resurrection of Jesus Christ from the dead to be saved?" Well, you cannot be saved without the Gospel, and it is a part of the Gospel. "I am not ashamed of the gospel of Christ," Paul wrote in Romans 1:16, "for it is the power of God unto salvation to every one that believeth; to the Jew first, and also to the Greek."

It is plainly taught in Romans 10:9 and 10 that you must "believe in thine heart that God hath raised him from the dead," if you are to be saved. So believing in the resurrection of Jesus Christ is a part of God's saving Gospel.

Now you follow the Apostle Paul in his great missionary journeys and his great program of evangelism, and you will see that Paul preached the resurrection of Jesus Christ as a necessity for the salvation of a lost soul. Acts 17:32 says, "And when they heard of the resurrection of the dead, some mocked: and others said, We will hear thee again of this matter." Then read verse 34: "Howbeit certain men clave unto him, and believed...."

So Paul preached in Athens that great sermon on Mars' Hill, on the subject of "The Resurrection of the Dead." When the people heard "the resurrection of the dead," there was a threefold response. Some mocked and said, "Why, we don't have to believe in the resurrection. That is not important. That doesn't matter. That doesn't mean anything to us." Others said, "Well, we are not sure. We are going to delay in making a decision about this; we are going to put it off. We are going to wait awhile; then we will make up our mind." But, thank God, there was a third class who believed and, as the Scripture says, "certain men clave unto him, and believed" and they were saved.

My friends, I say to you, you must believe in the bodily, literal resurrection of Jesus Christ, He who died on the cross robed in blood. You must believe that He arose in glorious power out of the grave. So you must believe in the resurrection of Jesus Christ as a part of the Gospel in order to be saved.

As I said it has been my wonderful privilege to visit many times, that most beautiful and lovely place called the Garden Tomb outside the City of Jerusalem, on the north side, where I firmly believe Jesus was buried, where the earthquake came, where the angels stood, where Jesus walked in triumph out of the grave and conquered death and lit the light of immortality in the grave forever. I have made most beautiful pictures and shown them often to large audiences in many places.

One night years ago, in this auditorium of the Emmanuel Baptist Church, someone was showing a beautiful colored picture of the empty tomb where the body of Jesus, wrapped in graveclothes, was laid after He died for the sins of the world upon the cross of Calvary. An unsaved man was sitting in the audience. He had been a hard case. He looked at that picture of the empty tomb, and the Gospel began to be made clear to him. The Spirit of God began to speak to him. The man began to see Calvary in its true light. He said to himself, "If that grave is empty, it means that God is satisfied with the death of Christ upon the cross; and if that tomb is empty, that means that He is on the throne and able to keep me forever. And if the tomb is empty, there is going to be a judgment day in which I must stand at the white throne judgment and give an account of my sins." That strong, big man came walking down the aisle weeping, and he was gloriously saved. He has been a wonderful testimony, a changed life for the Lord all these years. So the resurrection is a part of God's saving Gospel.

*"He shewed himself alive after his passion by many in-
fallible proofs...."—Acts 1:3.*

VII. The Physical Reality of the Resurrection

In the seventh place, I want you to see the physical reality
of the resurrection of Jesus Christ. Now those who do not
want to believe, those who want to deny it and destroy the
doctrine of the bodily, literal resurrection of Jesus from the
grave, have certain theories that they have proposed down
through the years in order to explain away the glorious doctrine of the resurrection of Jesus.

For instance, they say there was no burial in the first
place, that Jesus was never buried. Now this is ridiculous!
The Roman government handled the whole affair. They had
the tomb sealed and they saw that Jesus was dead. A centurion thrust a spear into Jesus' side, and did not break His
legs because it was not necessary; Jesus had already died.

And the Pharisees saw to it that Jesus was buried and a
watch set at the tomb. They went to Pilate and said:

*"Sir, we remember that that deceiver said, while he was
yet alive, After three days I will rise again. Command
therefore that the sepulchre be made sure until the third
day, lest his disciples come by night, and steal him away,
and say unto the people, He is risen from the dead: so the
last error shall be worse than the first. Pilate said unto
them, Ye have a watch: go your way, make it as sure as
ye can. So they went, and made the sepulchre sure, seal-
ing the stone, and setting a watch."—Matt. 27:63-66.*

It is true that the body of Jesus was given to Joseph of
Arimathaea, and he and Nicodemus, both believers, prepared it for burial. It was in Joseph's new-made tomb that
Jesus Christ was buried, there in that beautiful garden.
This is true, but there is no reason to believe that His body
was not buried at all. That would be a complete denial of
the Gospel of Jesus Christ, for the Gospel is that He died

for our sins according to the Scriptures, and that He was buried and on the third day He rose again according to the Scriptures. Some say there was no burial in the first place, but that is not true.

There are those who say that the body was stolen away instead of being raised from the dead by the power of God. Now this could not be true. You remember that they considered this before Jesus was ever entombed; and Pilate, the Roman governor, ordered the tomb sealed and a watch to be set before the stone that closed it. Here was a handful of defenseless Christians, and there were the Roman soldiers, backed by the Roman army; and a big stone was rolled in front of the grave and it was sealed by the Roman authorities, to see that Jesus did not arise and that His body was not stolen. Now, listen! All that does not make sense if there was no burial in the first place. How ridiculous to be guarding an empty tomb! Even His enemies testified that the body of Jesus Christ was placed in the grave. The evidence is that His body could not possibly have been stolen.

Then there is what is called the "Hallucination Theory." You know that for forty days after His resurrection, Jesus appeared only to believers. Not one unsaved person ever saw Him after His resurrection. During those forty days He made many appearances. In I Corinthians 15:5 and 6 we read that "he was seen of Cephas, then of the twelve: After that, he was seen of above five hundred brethren at once; of whom the greater part remain unto this present, but some are fallen asleep." He was seen by Cephas (that is, Simon Peter); one person saw Him. Had that been the only case, someone might have said, "Well, they wanted Him to arise so badly that they might have dreamed that He had, or they had an hallucination. They thought that He arose from the dead." But here are five hundred people. Now are you willing to believe—is it credible—that five hundred people had the same hallucination at the same time about the same thing? Now, that is incredible, that is unbelievable. The

hallucination theory is one of the most unbelievable and ridiculous ever pawned off on thinking people.

Then there is what is called the "Swoon Theory." That
is, Jesus was not really dead in the first place, they say.
The swoon theory has no basis, could not in fact be true,
One thing the executioner must be sure about is that the
malefactor is dead before he is ever removed from the
cross. Remember, they allowed Jesus to remain there for
a good many hours. Remember also that it was the Jews'
request that the legs of the victim be broken in order to be
sure that they were dead. Remember also that Jesus hung
on that cross after a sleepless night, without water, for at
least six hours. And when they came to break the legs of
the three—Jesus and the two thieves—they looked at Jesus
and said, "He is already dead. There is no question about
it." So they did not break His legs. The reason they didn't
is that the Bible says, "A bone of him shall not be broken"
(John 19:36), the fulfillment of a type of the passover lamb
of which it was commanded: "...neither shall ye break a
bone thereof" (Exod. 12:46). Not a bone of Jesus Christ was
to be broken. The Scriptures had to be fulfilled, so they
could not break His legs; He was already dead. The swoon
theory is not true. It is false. It is a lie of the Devil.

There is what is called a "Spiritual Resurrection." That
is that there was no bodily resurrection, no literal resurrection, no physical resurrection; that the resurrection of
Jesus was a spiritual resurrection only. Now if you will
think for a moment, you would see that this is not the truth.
In the first place, Jesus' spirit was not entombed in that
stone grave. You read Luke 23:46 and you will see that
Jesus said, "Father, into thy hands I commend my spirit."
He said, "Father, into thy hands...," not "into a tomb."
The Bible says, "And when Jesus had cried with a loud voice,
he said, Father, into thy hands I commend my spirit: and
having said thus, he gave up the ghost." Nothing could arise
from the grave that did not go into it in the first place. This

so-called teaching of a spiritual resurrection absolutely is not true. The resurrection of Jesus Christ was a physical resurrection. His body came out of the graveclothes and the napkin, neatly folded, was left at the head of the grave and the graveclothes in which He was wound were neatly left. An angel was there at the tomb and said, "Fear not ye: for I know that ye seek Jesus, which was crucified. He is not here: for he is risen, as he said. Come, see the place where the Lord lay" (Matt. 28:5,6). Thank God, Jesus' resurrection was a physical resurrection.

I read in I John 3:2 a glorious truth: "...we shall be like him; for we shall see him as he is." Now when Jesus comes and we are raised, we are going to have a body just like the body of Jesus Christ.

Paul also spoke of it in Philippians 3:21: "Who shall change our vile body, that it may be fashioned like unto his glorious body...." So this vile body of ours shall be made like that glorious body of His, physical, tangible, real body. We shall be like Him. The body of Jesus after the resurrection could be touched. He invited His disciples: "Behold my hands and my feet, that it is I myself: handle me, and see; for a spirit hath not flesh and bones, as ye see me have" (Luke 24:39). He could eat food. Luke 24:41-43 shows this: "And while they yet believed not for joy, and wondered, he said unto them, Have ye here any meat? And they gave him a piece of a broiled fish, and of an honeycomb. And he took it, and did eat before them." He could be seen on the shore, and could cook a meal at the Sea of Galilee for the disciples. This same Jesus, thank God, died on the cross, came out of the tomb, and some day is coming back to raise us from the dead, and make us like Him at last.

The physical reality of the resurrection of Jesus Christ! May God bless it to your hearts.

"He shewed himself alive after his passion [suffering] *by many infallible proofs, being seen of them forty days, and*

speaking of the things pertaining to the kingdom of God."—
Acts 1:3.

THE ASCENSION OF JESUS CHRIST

*"So then after the Lord had spoken unto them, he was re-
ceived up into heaven, and sat on the right hand of God. And
they went forth, and preached every where, the Lord working with them, and confirming the word with signs following."—Mark 16:19,20.*

I. The Ascension and a Finished Work of Redemption

II. The Ascension and a Constant Work of Intercession

III. The Ascension and the Great Commission

IV. The Ascension and Christian Service

V. The Ascension and Second Coming of Jesus Christ

VI. The Ascension and Answered Prayer

VII. The Ascension and a New Relationship

The Mount of Olives, seen from Jerusalem

"...this same Jesus, which is taken up from you into heaven, shall so come in like manner as ye have seen him go into heaven."—Acts 1:11.

8

The Ascension of Jesus Christ

"So then after the Lord had spoken unto them, he was re-
ceived up into heaven, and sat on the right hand of God. And
they went forth, and preached every where, the Lord work-
ing with them, and confirming the word with signs follow-
ing."—Mark 16:19,20.

There are seven great events in the earthly life and ministry of our Lord Jesus Christ. A great deal could be said
in distinguishing between the earthly ministry and the heavenly ministry of our blessed Lord. He is coexistent with
God and eternally existent with God. But I am talking about
the time that He was born in Bethlehem's manger and until
the time that He was received back into the presence of the
Father.

There are seven great events in the earthly ministry of
our Lord Jesus Christ. I briefly mention these to you because I want you to see the relationship of the subject of
this message with these other great events.

There was His miraculous birth. As you know, Jesus'
birth of a virgin woman, without an earthly father, is called
the virgin birth. There was the incarnation, when Jesus
tabernacled His deity within the confines of a little baby
body. Luke 2:11 speaks of this: "For unto you is born this
day in the city of David a Saviour, which is Christ the
Lord." There is His vicarious, atoning death upon the
cross of Calvary. Romans 5:6 says, "For when we were
yet without strength, in due time Christ died for the ungodly." Third, there is His glorious, triumphant resurrection
of Christ out of the grave. First Corinthians 15:20 says,

"But now is Christ risen from the dead, and become the firstfruits of them that slept."

Fourth, and the subject of this message, is the ascension of Jesus Christ. Luke 24:51 says, "And it came to pass, while he blessed them, he was parted from them, and carried up into heaven."

Fifth, there is the second coming of Christ. Revelation 1:7 says, "Behold, he cometh with clouds; and every eye shall see him, and they also which pierced him: and all kindreds of the earth shall wail because of him."

Sixth, there is the transfiguration of Jesus Christ. In my thirty-some odd years of preaching, I do not believe that I have ever heard a sermon preached on the transfiguration of Christ. Matthew 17:2 says, "And was transfigured before them: and his face did shine as the sun, and his raiment was white as the light."

In the seventh place, we have the baptism by immersion of Jesus Christ by John the Baptist. Matthew 3:16 says, "And Jesus, when he was baptized, went up straightway out of the water: and, lo, the heavens were opened unto him, and he saw the Spirit of God descending like a dove, and lighting upon him."

We have seen the seven great doctrinal events in the life and earthly ministry of Jesus Christ. But in this message I want to deal mainly with the ascension of our Lord Jesus Christ.

The ascension is mentioned in all the first five books of the New Testament except the book of Matthew. I do not know why Matthew does not discuss the ascension, but Mark, Luke, John and the book of Acts all deal with the tremendous event in the earthly ministry of our Lord Jesus Christ—His ascension, back in the Glory in the presence of the Father.

As all of you know, from the time that He arose from the dead and ascended back into the presence of the Father, Jesus spent forty days upon this earth. During those forty days He never appeared to a single unsaved person. From the time that they took Him off the cross until He ascended back into the presence of the Father, we understand that no unconverted person ever laid eyes on Jesus Christ. The last picture this world ever had of the Son of God was when they saw Him hanging on the cross, crowned with thorns, bleeding and dying. So for forty days after His crucifixion, and until His ascension, He appeared only to saved people.

He appeared to as few as one, like Mary as I mentioned, and to as many as five hundred people in His resurrected body, during these forty days. Jesus made at least a dozen appearances during these forty days. So people ask, "Why forty days?"

I do not exactly know why, but I do know there is a special significance to the number forty in the Bible. Some have said that forty always has to do with testing and with proof and assurance and certainty.

For instance, forty days and forty nights was Moses on the mountaintop; forty years was Israel in the wilderness led of God; forty years Moses spent in the backside of the desert; Nineveh was given forty days to repent; Jesus was tempted forty days and forty nights without a drop of water or a morsel of bread; Elijah did not eat for forty days after he was fed with food provided by God's angel (I Kings 19:8). All through the Bible, forty is a time of testing.

So for forty days and forty nights Jesus appeared between His crucifixion at Calvary and His ascension back into glory. When you study His being taken up into the presence of God after His death, after His resurrection, after His forty days' appearing, you will find that His ascension is linked in the Bible with many great doctrines that are dear to our hearts. It is also related to many truths put forth in the Bible. It is inseparably related to many other events recorded in the ministry of Jesus Christ. This is an important event, the ascension of Jesus back into the presence of the Father.

I have picked out of the Scriptures at least seven things related to the ascension of Jesus Christ back into the presence of the Father in a visible, literal, tangible, physical body.

"He was received up into heaven."—Mark 16:19.

I. The Ascension and a Finished Work of Redemption

First of all, notice the ascension of Jesus and a finished work of redemption. Our text tells us that He was taken up into Heaven and sat on the right hand of God. If you will think about it, even that picture indicates something that He came to earth to do. That picture itself, "sat down at the right hand of God," would indicate that He had finished something planned in the councils of God before the beginning of time. Hebrews 1:3 says, "...when he had by himself purged our sins, sat down on the right hand of the Majesty on high."

Go through the Old Testament and you will see many types and figures, all of which speak of Jesus Christ. There is no more wonderful thing in the Old Testament that speaks of Jesus than the Tabernacle in the wilderness or the Temple built by Solomon. In that Tabernacle there was the holy of holies. There was the outer court, there was the inner court, and there was the holy of holies. You read in the book of Exodus and Leviticus and find that not twice or three times, but only once a year did the high priest go into the holy of holies with blood.

In that holy of holies was the ark of the covenant, a small box about the size of a communion table. It was overlaid inside and out with gold. There were three articles found inside, which speak of something. There were the tablets of the law; there was a golden pot full of heavenly manna and there was Aaron's almond rod that bloomed and budded to which God had given life. When that was closed, the lid of that ark of covenant made up what was called the mercy seat which is mentioned many times in the Old and New

Testament—the mercy seat in the holy of holies. The high priest would come with a basin of blood in one hand and incense in the other and seven times would he dip his finger in the blood and seven times sprinkle it upon the ark of the covenant, the mercy seat, in the holy of holies.

Study the furniture of the Tabernacle, the outer court, the inner court, the holy of holies, and you will find tables, equipment of all kinds, the tools that the priests used, the flesh hook, the shovels; you will find places for fire to burn, you will find the tables—but one thing you will never find is a chair. The priest never sat down. His work was never finished. He never got through. He continued to sprinkle the blood. Year by year he would go beyond the veil and out of sight of the people and sprinkle the blood upon the mercy seat, but he never sat down. He never got through. His work was never finished because it was constantly, continually, perpetually, always pointing to the coming of the Lamb of God, slain from the foundations of the world.

When Jesus was dying on the cross, seven times He opened His mouth to speak and one time He uttered—in the original language, one word; in the English translation, three words—but only one word Jesus uttered on the cross, "Finished!" He cried until it shook the world. He cried until Heaven heard Him. "Finished!" It is all done. "'Tis done! 'Tis done! The great transaction's done!" The work of grace and love and salvation was gloriously completed in the death of Jesus Christ. No wonder when John saw Him he said, "...Behold the Lamb of God, which taketh away the sin of the world."

The blood upon the mercy seat covered sin over waiting for Jesus to come. But the blood of Jesus that was shed on the cross and gathered in a crimson pool washed it away forever, thank God!

This Bible teaches that He has removed our sins as far as the east is from the west. He has blotted them out as a thick cloud. He has put them behind His back. He has forgotten them, to remember them against us no more forever. Hallelujah! We can look back to a finished work.

I do not have to say like Abraham said, "When will Jesus come?" I will not have to say like Isaac said, "When will Jesus come? When will God's Lamb appear?" I thank God that I can look back over nineteen hundred years of glorious history and see yonder an empty tomb and a bloody cross, and I can cry like Jesus cried, "It is finished"! The sin question has been settled. The ascension is related to the finished work of redemption, when He was taken back into the presence of the Father.

I will illustrate with this story I heard back when the Salvation Army people used to stand on the street corners. There was a day when the Army was not just playing the bands and collecting money, but one of the greatest evangelistic movements the world has ever known in the history of the church was that of the Salvation Army. From every street corner and gutter, from every ghetto and slum area around the world there was the Salvation Army—men and women telling the story of Christ and people being saved. It is not so today. Like many other religious groups, they have gone the way of liberalism and modernism and are in social service instead of gospel preaching.

There was a man standing on the curb preaching. The drunks, the gamblers, the harlots, the libertines were all there. They listened and people were being saved. It is said that one man knelt right in the gutter, clasped his hands together, looked up toward Heaven with his eyes closed and cried, "What shall I do? What shall I do? What shall I do about my sins? What shall I do? What shall I do about my soul? What shall I do? What shall I do?"

The Salvation Army worker, who wanted him to get it straight and see it clearly, reached down and touched him on his head and said, "Too late! Too late! You can't do anything."

He said the man lifted up his head and with a hopeless

stare in his sin-scarred face, said, "Too late? Too late? What can I do? What can I do?"

The Salvation Army man said, "Thank God! You do not have to do anything. It has all been done! It is finished!" It is finished. Christ did it all. He paid sin's debt. He turned the cup of God's holy wrath and drank the very dregs of it and finished your sin's debt and paid the penalty of your sins. All you can do is believe, accept, receive. You can't work it out. You can't pay for it. You will never deserve it. Just accept it—that is all."

"What can I do?" he said.

"Just believe and receive. It is a finished work."

So when the Bible speaks of the ascension of Jesus back into the presence of the Father, it shows that He sat down, His work of redemption being finished.

"He was received up into heaven."—Mark 16:19.

II. The Ascension and a Constant Work of Intercession

In the second place, notice the ascension of Jesus Christ and a constant work of intercession. Notice again in our text, "...and sat down on the right hand of God." That is where He is at this moment. How I wish I could paint the picture to you and get you to see what it means for you and for me that Jesus not only died on a cross, not only walked out of a cold, stone tomb, but thank God, this moment He is at God's right hand interceding for you and me! The ascension and the constant work of intercession.

You see it a number of times in the Bible. In fact, Stephen mentioned this, that first deacon who preached that great sermon in Acts 7, and was stoned to death for His preaching. As he was dying, we read, "Behold, I see the heavens opened, and the Son of man standing on the right hand of God" (Acts 7:56). Stephen, when nearer Heaven than earth, with life ebbing out, crossing the great divide between life here and life over there, said the heavens are opening.

I have known of saints who have said it. A dear old lady

died, a member of the Emmanuel Baptist Church. On the morning that she died, she said to her husband, "Open that window." (He told Mrs. Malone and me about it in the home a few minutes after she died.) She said, "Open the window." He opened the window and all on her own strength she turned over so that she could look out the open window. All of a sudden she said, "There He is! There He is!" and closed her eyes and left this earthly scene and went out to be with the Saviour.

That is what Stephen saw. "...I see the heavens opened, and the Son of man standing on the right hand of God."

If I had the time I would like to deal more on the three men in the Bible who saw Him there. Stephen saw Him there when he died. Saul saw Him there when he was converted. John saw Him there when he was exiled on that rocky little Isle of Patmos and had the Revelation given to him. He is at the right hand of God.

You ask, "What does that mean—Jesus at God's right hand?" Oh, what wonderful things it really means. In I John 2:1 I read these words, "My little children, these things write I unto you, that ye sin not. And if any man sin, we have an advocate with the Father, Jesus Christ the righteous." It means that when you sin after you are saved, you do not lose your soul, you do not lose your home in Heaven, and you do not lose your standing before God. It never changes. Your state does; your standing doesn't. Why? Because of His advocacy, His intercessory work, His mediatorial ministry at the throne of God. He is at God's right hand.

Notice it again in Hebrews 9:24: "...now to appear in the presence of God for us." Look at the last two words. How glad I am that they are in the Bible. "Now to appear in the presence of God FOR US." Jesus, why are you there? For me, for you, my friends, "Now to appear in the presence of God FOR US."

I would like for you to look at a verse that I think has

been misinterpreted more than any verse, perhaps, in all the Bible. Hebrews 7:25 says, "Wherefore he is able also to save them to the uttermost that come unto God by him, seeing he ever liveth to make intercession for them." Oh, how many times I have heard that verse quoted! I have heard people say, "He is able to save from the guttermost to the uttermost," and He is. But that is not what this means. I have heard them say, "Oh, Jesus is able to reach down to the very deepest depths of sin and save people," and He is. But that is not what it means.

He is able to save to the uttermost. It is not how far down He reaches; it is how far out His salvation goes. It means that He is able to save to the uttermost—to the end; to the fartherest extremity. While the ages roll, while eternity goes on and on and on, Jesus, thank God, keeps His people saved. He is able to save to the fartherest extremity all those who come unto God by Him. Why? "...seeing he ever liveth to make intercession for them"—for us! For us in the presence of God.

I want you to notice something else. The reason so many Christians are up one day and down the next is that they have never learned the difference between "state" and "standing." State is the way you are right now. There may be something between you and God.

State changes from day to day. Tomorrow you may get prayed up and cleaned up before God through Bible reading and confession of sins. Your state may change from day to day. But standing never changes. Standing is your relationship to God through the ministry of Jesus at the right hand of the throne in Glory and it never, never changes, the Bible teaches.

Romans 5:10 says, "For if, when we were enemies, we were reconciled to God by the death of his Son, much more, being reconciled, we shall be saved by his life." What does "We shall be saved by his life" mean? I have had people say, "Now doesn't this prove that it was not necessary that blood be shed, not necessary that Jesus die for you to be saved? Doesn't this say, 'We shall be saved by his life'?" That is not what it means.

I have heard people say, "Since Jesus never did wrong, and since He was right with others, right with God, true to Himself, doesn't it mean that if we follow His example, His life, walk in His steps, we will be saved by His life on earth?" That is not the life He is talking about. It is not His life yonder side of the cross, it is not His life yonder side of the tomb. It is His life this side of the cross, this side of the tomb. At the throne, in the Glory, "We shall be saved by his life," at the right hand of God. The literal interpretation is that we were reconciled to God by His death and we are kept saved by His life—the ascension of Jesus Christ and a constant work of intercession.

I want you to notice something. You see the matter of being kept saved applied in the Bible again and again. I have had people say to me, "Preacher, if I knew I could live it, I would get saved." You had better not wait on that. You are never going to know that while standing on the other side. You are never going to know that while you are in the dark. You are never going to know that while standing in the Devil's kingdom.

I have had people say, "Why, if I knew I could live it...." Let me tell you, you can't live it. But I will tell you Someone who can. Jesus can, in you! He can, in you.

I have also had people say, "Oh, if I could stay saved...." One day Jesus spoke to Simon Peter. Now no one doubts that Simon Peter was a Christian. I know that Peter was saved. With his sins and failures, his repentance and tears, the whole Bible shows Simon Peter was a Christian, was born again, before Jesus ever died on the cross. He was gloriously, wonderfully saved and called and Peter was a great preacher. One day Jesus said to Simon Peter, recorded in Luke 22:31,32, "Simon, behold, Satan hath desired to have you...." I can say to any man, woman, boy or girl in this day and age, Satan hath desired to have you. Satan wants you. He will ruin you. He wants to mess up your life. He wants to cloud up your mind. He wants you to get mixed up on the real truth and what it means to be saved. "Satan hath desired to have you that he may sift you as wheat: But I have prayed for thee [talking to Simon Peter], that thy faith fail not: and when thou art converted [not saved, but when thou art turned back again], strengthen thy brethren."

Jesus said, "Peter, Satan hath desired to get you, but I have prayed for thee, that thy faith fail not, and you will always come back to God because you are saved." That is what He said. That is what I believe. This Bible teaches that you are saved by His death on the cross of Calvary, and kept by His life at the throne in the Glory.

He ascended back into the presence of the Father, and He is at the right hand of God.

Hebrews 4:14 is one of the greatest verses in the Bible on this subject! "Seeing then that we have a great high priest, that is passed into the heavens [that is the ascension], Jesus the Son of God, let us hold fast our profession." Now notice the next two verses: "For we have not an high priest which cannot be touched with the feeling of our infirmities; but was in all points tempted like as we are, yet without sin. Let us therefore come boldly unto the throne of grace, that we may obtain mercy, and find grace to help in time of need."

You see, God said that you have an Advocate at the throne, a Go-between between you and the Father. You have a Lawyer for your case. You have a Daysman who has put His hand on you and the other on God and is forever there. The Bible says He is touched by whatever touches you. He feels what you feel; He hurts when you hurt; He weeps when you weep; He is concerned with all that touches you. "We have not an high priest which cannot be touched with the feeling of our infirmities."

There are some four or five wonderful truths that I wish

I had time to deal with in detail. First of all, there is Someone at the throne. He is touched and He feels. He knows our every trial, gives us grace for every need, sees that our prayers are answered. Oh, a sympathetic Saviour, now at the right hand of God!

Dr. Bob Jones, Sr.—God bless his sainted memory—used to often tell of something that happened on a train many years ago. On a Pullman car one night, a man walked the aisle most of the evening with a crying little child. About two or three o'clock in the morning, a man stuck his head out of one of the berths in the Pullman car and hollered very loudly and bluntly, "Stop that child from crying! Give it to its mother!" It is said that the man continued to pace up and down the aisle with the little baby in his arms. In a bit he walked to where the man had parted the curtains of his berth and very tenderly and politely, and with big tears rolling down his face, said, "I wish to God that I could give her to her mother! But you see, Sir, the little child's mother, my good wife, is in the baggage car in her casket. We are taking the little child and her mother, my good wife, back to her hometown, the scene of her childhood where she soon will be buried. I would give anything in this world if I could give the child back to her mother."

It is said that in a moment there came climbing out of another berth a man who had put on his robe and slippers. He walked up to this man, reached out his arms and said, "Go get some rest. Let me walk the aisles with your child, this motherless baby. For a few years ago one dark day death came and took the mother of my children, the wife of my life. I know what it means. I have been mother and dad to my little children and I know what it means to have a child weep for her mother. Let me carry her. I understand."

Oh, thank God, there is a Saviour who one day walked back up an invisible golden stairway and into the presence of God and took up a work at the throne. He looks down upon every single Christian. He knows every tear you shed. He knows every sigh that comes from your sobbing breast. He knows every heartache. He sees you when you walk through every hot fire of temptation. We have at the throne a Priest, a High Priest, thank God, who can be touched with the feeling of our infirmities.

"He was received up into heaven, and sat down on the right hand of God."—Mark 16:19.

III. The Ascension and the Great Commission

There is in the Word of God the teaching of the ascension and the Great Commission. They are linked together. I do not know of anything more important than what I am going to say to you in the next few moments. I do not know of anything about which more churches fail than the ascension and the Great Commission. I relate back to my text "...he was received up into heaven, and sat on the right hand of God. And they went forth, and preached every where, the Lord working with them, and confirming the word with signs following." So here the ascension is inseparably linked with the marching orders of the church.

A verse in the Bible, speaking of man and wife, "What God hath joined together, let no man put asunder," is true of this doctrine. "What God has joined together in truth, don't ever let any one divide." The ascension and the Great Commission are linked together. "...they went forth, and preached every where."

You will notice in the Bible the power of the Great Commission. In Matthew 28:18 Jesus said, "All power is given unto me in heaven and in earth." In Acts 1:8 He said, "But ye shall receive power, after that the Holy Ghost is come upon you: and ye shall be witnesses unto me both in Jerusalem, and in all Judaea, and in Samaria, and unto the uttermost part of the earth."

Notice the program of the Great Commission. Luke 24: 47,48 says, "And that repentance and remission of sins should be preached in his name among all nations, beginning at Jerusalem. And ye are witnesses of those things." That is the program. To all nations. Listen, a church that sits still is not a New Testament church. A church that does not shake every bush in the city and knock on every door in town, plus sending the Gospel across the ocean to the remote corners of the world, is not doing what Jesus said to do.

I want you to notice the plan of the Great Commission. What does it all mean? Some people say, "All it means is just to get people saved." But that is not all it means. That is not all the work of the church. In this Great Commission in Matthew the 28th chapter, Jesus said, "All power is given unto me in heaven and in earth. Go ye therefore, and teach ...."

Now you say, "Why did the Lord say teach first?" Well, that word means disciple. It means get people to sit down and listen to Jesus and believe in Him, be saved and become a follower of Him. It is just another way of saying, "Get people saved." "Go ye therefore, and teach [disciple] all nations [what is next?], baptizing them in the name of the Father, and of the Son, and of the Holy Ghost [What is next?]: Teaching them [all things that I have taught you. What is next?] to observe [practice it, too] all things whatsoever I have commanded you [What is next? The presence of the Great Commission. Jesus said when you do this you can always depend on one thing]: and, lo, I am with you alway, even unto the end of the world."

I see in this text the performance of the Great Commission. We read, "And they went forth." Oh, my friend, may I encourage you, may I beg of you, may I implore you, may I pressure you, go forth! That is what Jesus said do. "And they went forth, and preached every where!"

I think of what a native, who had never before heard about Jesus, said to a missionary on the field some years ago. This is supposed to have happened. The missionary told him that Jesus, the Son of God, member of the Trinity, came from the glory of Heaven to this earth and walked among men and died upon a cross, died that every man, regardless of color, might be saved, and that if one believed in Him, he could be a Christian.

The native believed the message of the Gospel and was wondrously saved, then he said, "I want to ask you this question: Where have you been? Where have you Christians been for 1900 years? Where have you been?"

The missionary said, "What do you mean?"

The native said, "No one has ever come to our village before. No one here has ever heard of Jesus Christ before. Where have you Christians been? Where have you been since Jesus went back to the Father?"

I wonder how many neighbors and citizens of Pontiac and America are asking, "Where have you Christians been?" He went up, that we may go out! And if we do not go out, we frustrate the holy purpose for which He went back to the Father.

The ascension and the Great Commission.

"He was received up into heaven, and sat on the right hand of God. And they went forth and preached every where."
—*Mark 16:19,20.*

IV. The Ascension and Christian Service

In the fourth place there is the ascension and Christian service. Ephesians 4:8 says, "When he ascended up on high, he led captivity captive, and gave gifts unto men." "When he ascended up on high [that is His ascension], he led captivity captive, and gave gifts unto men."

Notice that this passage teaches that God through an ascended Christ gives gifts unto men wherewith they ought to serve Him. I read something here in this passage that I believe every Christian needs to earnestly contemplate and heed. Everyone, not just preachers, not just Christian leaders, not people with talent and ability, but every Christian, through an ascended Lord, has the ability to serve the Lord Jesus Christ. It says, "Unto every one of us." Not just preachers, not evangelists alone, not just missionaries, not just people who can sing, but "Unto every one of us is given grace according to the measure of the gift of Christ" (Eph. 4:7). That teaches that every single child of God, through an ascended Lord, has the responsibility, through the Holy Spirit of God, to find out what that gift is.

I believe with all my heart that I am called to preach. Not by men, not by the church, not by my friends, but I believe through an ascended Lord, I have been called to preach. That is my calling. The Bible does not teach that just some are called to serve, but that all are given a gift of some kind through which they can serve the Lord. That is what it means when it says, "He ascended on high, he led captivity captive, and gave gifts unto men." So His ascension has to do with Christian service.

Then it has to do with something else. This Christian service is for the edification of the church of Jesus Christ. I want you to notice in this passage that it teaches that "for the perfecting of the saints, for the work of the ministry, for the edifying of the body of Christ" (Eph. 4:12). Something that needs to be taught today is a reverence for the body of Jesus Christ, that is, that saved group of born-again, blood-washed people of God. A holy love for them ought to be taught. God says, "All that we do is to edify that body" which is joined to the Head. Woe be unto the man or woman who professes to be a Christian and does anything devisive or destructive to that body. God says that all this, through an ascended Christ, is for the edification, the up-building of the body of Christ. It would make a difference when we preach, teach, sing, usher, if we would say, "It is through a Jesus that ascended into Heaven I have been given a gift wherewith I can serve and edify the body of Christ."

Years ago there was a fruit peddler who was a wonderful

Christian. He pushed a little cart around and sold fruit. He carried a Bible, but he also carried a little black book besides. That was all the man had in his pocket, we are told. They said every once in a while he would take out that little black book and write something in it. People used to wonder what he wrote in that little black book. No one ever got to see it.

One day a car hit him and knocked him down. The accident injured him seriously and later the man died. Out of his belongings came his Bible and his little black book. That little black book was filled with things like this. It had a verse that said, "For his body's sake, which is the church." Then under that was written things he had to do. He had made a note that on Tuesday, "I must take groceries to the widow and her children." On Wednesday, "I must visit the little crippled boy." He had made the note, "For his body's sake, which is the church." On Friday, "I must visit a family that is having family trouble." Then the note, "For his body's sake, which is the church."

My friends, spiritual Christians have gifts that they can use to edify the church of Jesus Christ. Oh, you may be like I was when I was saved. I said, "I have no talent." I said, "I cannot sing." I said, "I am not real smart. What will I do?" When one surrenders to God with all his heart, I think Jesus on the throne, through the blessed Holy Ghost, says, "I will use this in that person, or that in this person."

I met a man one time before I walked into a church who had a great big smile on his face. With a great big hand, twice as big as mine, he grabbed my hand, shook it, looked me right in the face, smiled, welcomed me and said, "I was saved in there. When I got saved, I asked myself the question, 'What in the world can I do for Jesus Christ?' I am not educated, I have no talent." Then he said, "One day I made up my mind that I was going to be the best 'handshaker' this church has ever had. I am going to make people feel that when they walk through these doors something real and wonderful is taking place. I made up my mind that I would never let anyone be a better 'handshaker' than I."

He shook my hand and told me that story and I couldn't wait to get to the pulpit and preach. I thank God for a Christian who is searching his mind, searching his heart, going to his knees and looking for something to do in some way to serve Christ and edify the body of Christ.

The ascension of Jesus Christ and Christian service.

"When he ascended on high...he gave gifts unto men." — *Eph. 4:8.*

V. The Ascension and Second Coming of Jesus Christ

Now in the fifth place you will notice in the Bible the ascension of Jesus Christ and His second coming. Here are two things that are not separated in the Scripture. You remember in Acts 1:10,11 when the Lord ascended near the Mount of Olives just in the presence of His own, as He went up, two men in white apparel came down and said, "This same Jesus, which is taken up from you into heaven, shall so come in like manner as ye have seen him go into heaven."

In that chapter you find four times where God emphasizes, "He is taken up. He is taken up. He is taken up. He is taken up." He is going to come back just exactly as He was taken up. God was careful to send two angels down and say to all who stood there and all of us now, "Just like He went away, just like He was taken up and ascended into Heaven, He will descend some day to take the church Home."

He went away bodily, and that is the way He is coming back. Many people think of the second coming of Christ as just a doctrine or some spiritual truth. But the second coming, my friends, is a reality. He is coming back in a body that is visible. He went away suddenly; He is coming back suddenly. He went away in the presence of His own; He is coming just for His own. He went away in blessing with His hands outstretched; He is coming back for His own the same way: to raise the dead, to translate the living, to unite them together, to catch them up with Himself. He is coming back just like He ascended. He is going to descend.

I believe in connection with this, God in His Word makes it clear what He is doing in the age in which you and I are privileged to live. Acts 15:14 says, "Simeon hath declared how God at the first did visit the Gentiles [This expression is found only one time in the Bible and this tells you what it is all about, what the work of God is, what the church is supposed to do, what Christians ought to be interested in], to take out of them a people for his name."

Now, between the ascension and the second coming, God has a purpose and that purpose is to take out of this earth those who believe and make them a people for His name. When that group is completed—no sooner, no later—the Lord is going to come.

I have often thought how wonderful if some Sunday morning when the invitation is given and when the Spirit of God is speaking and people are walking these aisles to be saved, like they do every Lord's Day in the Emmanuel Baptist Church, some man, woman, boy or girl would come down the aisle and take this preacher by the hand and just as that one said, "I believe in Jesus Christ"—he would be the one to finish that group of "people for his name." And yonder in Heaven Jesus would say, "It is time to go," and from Heaven to earth He would come to take His people Home.

Yes, He ascended that He might return again. The ascension of Jesus Christ is linked with the second coming of Jesus Christ.

There was a wonderful man, Dr. John Roach Stratton. He was once a pastor of Calvary Baptist Church in New York City. Even while he was in the ministry, Dr. Stratton used to smoke. I have often said that there are worse things than smoking, but I am absolutely positive that there are a lot better things. I have made up my mind not to give the cigarette smokers the devil all the time and miss saying something to these old long-tongued gossipers, who are worse. I do take my stand on tobacco. I do believe a Christian can be a better Christian by not being a cigarette smoker. I believe he will have a better testimony.

Someone asked one time, "Do you believe a man can go to Heaven and chew tobacco?" The answer was, "Yeah, but you will have to go down to Hell to spit!"

Someone once said, "Do you believe a Christian can smoke and go to Heaven?" The answer was, "Yes, and a lot sooner!" I believe that, too.

One day while smoking a cigarette, the thought came to Dr. Stratton, "A Christian should ever live in the light of the coming of the Lord. And a Christian should be sure that his life is pleasing to God. Suppose the Lord came and found me with one in my hand." It is said that John Roach Stratton threw the cigarette down and thinking of the ascended Jesus coming again, said, "I will never again grieve my Lord by taking that poison in my body."

So you have the ascension and the second coming of Jesus Christ.

"He was received up into heaven."—Mark 16:19.

VI. The Ascension and Answered Prayer

In the sixth place, there is the ascension and answered prayer. I never realized before how many things are connected in the Bible to the up-taking of our Lord after He had finished His work on earth. You find that even answered prayer is connected with the ascension of Jesus.

Now notice this. I never thought until recently about it this way. I have studied about Pentecost and about the promise of Jesus, that the Holy Spirit would come. But did you ever stop and think that one of the greatest guarantees that God answers prayer is right in this thing?

For instance, Jesus said in John 14:16, "And I will pray the Father, and he shall give you another Comforter, that he may abide with you for ever." He said, "I am going to

pray that when I go up, when I ascend, another Comforter—
the Holy Ghost—will come down." On the day of Pentecost
the Holy Spirit came down. Ten days after Jesus went up,
the Holy Ghost came down, and Christians must have said,
"Thank God, He answers prayer." Jesus said, "I am going
to pray that another will come." He has come and it proves
that God answers prayer.

I thank God for the miracle of answered prayer. I say to
you, friends, I believe in a God who can do supernatural
things through the prayers of God's people. I have seen God
do it. I have had God do it for me. I have had God work
miracles in my life that are so delicate, yet so wonderful
that I am almost reluctant to even refer to them. But God
is a miracle-working God. God, my friends, answers the
prayers of people who pray for a clean heart and believe
His promises. Jesus said, "When I go, I am going to pray
that God will send another." Pentecost is a proof that God
answers prayer. Oh, thank God for answered prayer!

Talking about this "God is dead" foolishness: it is such
a ridiculous discussion that it is hardly worth talking about.
"Is God dead?" That is the most ridiculous thing in the
world. Only someone with a "fluffy" head could ever discuss something like that. Someone asked a lady what she
thought about it. She answered, "I know that He isn't dead."

"How do you know?"

"Because I just talked to Him this morning!"

God answers prayer!

I was reading recently in the Old Testament about the
high priest who went once a year to the holy of holies.
There is a beautiful picture there, a wonderfully blessed
thing to study about. A whole chapter in the Bible tells how
the priest should be dressed. He had on his robe and ephod
and all that; and I began to read about what was on the bottom of that robe. It says that there was a "golden bell and a
pomegranate, a golden bell and a pomegranate" upon the
hem of the robe, around the bottom of it (Exod. 28:34). God

said to put a little golden tinkling bell and a pomegranate and another bell and a pomegranate all the way around.

Then the next verse explains why. That the people may know He is in there ministering. The little bells keep ringing. He is sprinkling the blood on the mercy seat. He is making the intercession. He is the interceder, the intercessor between them and God. All the time the little bells are ringing the people outside are saying, "He is still alive. He still intercedes. He still pleads our cause. He is still in there. He still applies the blood."

That is what happens when a Christian prays. You hear the bells ringing, and He answers you and you know He is still alive, at the mercy seat in the Glory. So the ascension of Jesus is connected with answered prayer.

I wonder how many of the Lord's people really enjoy and experience a prayer life.

I read a story recently about a man and his son who were traveling with a large amount of money. Back in the olden days when people traveled across country, they would go and ask for a place to stay at night. There were no motels or hotels then. So they came to a home. The total stranger said, "Yes, you can spend the night here." The father said to his son, "Now one of us will sleep and the other one will watch. Who knows! These people may steal the money." The son was to do the watching first.

The father went to sleep. In a few minutes the son got in bed and was almost asleep, when the father said, "I thought you were going to watch until the midnight hour."

The son replied, "There is no need to watch."

The father said, "How do you know?"

The son said, "While I was waiting and watching there at the door, I saw the old man of the house get out an old black Bible. He opened it and began to read about loving your neighbor and loving the Lord. Dad, I saw those two old people get down on their knees in this home and pray. Dad, you don't need to worry. People who pray won't steal your money."

People who know that God answers prayers and pray about things, live right because there is no other way to get God to answer your prayers except through a clean heart.

So the ascension of Jesus is the guarantee that God answers prayer.

"He was received up into heaven."—Mark 16:19.

VII. The Ascension and a New Relationship

In the seventh place, the ascension means a new relationship. Some years ago I read where some man said that the ascension is not mentioned in Matthew or John. As I began to read and study the subject recently, I thought of that remark. But I got a big shock. I found out that "big commentaries" sometimes don't know what they are talking about. John has a lot to say about the ascension of Jesus Christ.

In John 20:17,18, it is recorded that after He arose from the dead, Mary Magdalene, out of whom He had cast seven devils, came to Him in the garden but did not recognize Him. She said, thinking that He was the gardener, "They have taken away my Lord, and I do not know what has happened to Him." Jesus, on the morning of the resurrection, turned to her and said, "Mary." You know Jesus said, "My sheep know my voice." And she was one of them. She knew that voice. She turned and said, "Rabboni," or "Master." She knew then it was Jesus, and she fell down at His feet and started to lay her arms around His feet, which was an act of worship in Bible days, but Jesus said to her, "Touch me not; for I am not yet ascended to my Father: but go to my brethren, and say unto them, I ascend unto my Father, and your Father; and to my God, and your God" (John 20:17,18).

Here Jesus talks to Mary about the fact, "Don't touch me now because I am not yet officially ascended."

What does that mean? It means the relationship. It means what Paul said in I Corinthians 5:16, "Wherefore henceforth know we no man after the flesh: yea, though we have known Christ after the flesh, yet now henceforth know we him no more." It is not knowing Christ after the flesh. It is not knowing Him physically by sight but spiritually by faith. He is teaching Mary that when He goes back to the Father, there is going to be a relationship between Himself and believers that is sweeter and stronger and more wonderful than they had had with Him. "You have seen Me sit at the table; You have sat at My feet; You have listened to My words; You have seen Me work miracles, but I know something better. When I go back to the Father there is going to be a spiritual union and relationship that I will always maintain because I am at the throne." He said, "Mary, don't touch me now. From now on it is not a relationship of the flesh, but it is a spiritual relationship. It is by faith, not by sight."

I have often had people ask, "How do you know that there is a God? Have you ever seen Him?" No, but I have talked to Him. I have come to know Him, if I may say so, intimately. I have come to love Him as I have never loved anyone else. I have come to feel His heartbeat as I never felt any other. I have never laid eyes on Him physically, but just like the Bible says, it is a spiritual relationship. It is not a fleshly one now like Mary and the disciples had. We walk by faith, not by sight.

I read something else in John. I took this verse many times in my ministry and tried to prepare a sermon on it but I couldn't. I don't know whether I ever will or not. It is so great that I don't understand it. I can't sound its depth. It is a verse I stand and look at in amazement. I know it is true. I believe it with all my heart.

In John 14:12 Jesus said, "Verily, verily, I say unto you, He that believeth on me, the works that I do shall he do also; and greater works than these shall he do; because I go unto my Father." The ascension! He said, "Because I go to my Father, the works that I do, you shall do also." If the Lord didn't say any more than that, I still would have trouble figuring it out. If He would have said, "The work that I do, you are going to do," I still would be standing off looking at that verse saying, "Lord, I don't understand how we are going to do what You did." But that is what He said, "He that believeth on me, the works that I do shall he do also."

But He went so much further than that. He just absolutely put me in a puzzle when He said, "And greater works than these shall he do; because I go unto my Father." I don't understand it all. I have read where great Bible scholars have said: "It is apostolic. It means the apostles will do it." I don't believe that it means that only. I think whatever it means, it includes me. If I could find out what it means, then I would know how to apply it to me. But He said, "Because I go to my Father, the work that I do shall you also, and even greater."

I do know this. I know that some of the miracles Jesus did had to do with material things. The bread and fish from which He fed the five thousand, soon went back to decay and corruption. What we are doing now is a work that will never know an end. It may be that is what Jesus meant. When He turned the water to wine not long after that—it all disappeared and the people who took part in it have all died and gone. What I am doing now and what you are doing now will live as long as God does. When someone gets saved and his name is written in the Lamb's Book of Life, there will be no end to that. Could that be what Jesus meant when He said, "The works that I do shall he do also; and greater works"? Why? "Because I go unto my Father."

Jesus ascending at God's right hand really means something to a Christian.

Then I found something else in John in spite of commentaries. Jesus said, "Let not your heart be troubled: ye believe in God, believe also in me. In my Father's house are many mansions: if it were not so, I would have told you. I go to prepare a place for you. [The ascension.] And if I go and prepare a place for you, I will come again, and receive you unto myself; that where I am, there ye may be also."

That is the new relationship of a Christian and the hope of Heaven. I wonder if you have that—the hope of Heaven? I have the hope of Heaven. Do you? Jesus said, "I am going to ascend." The reason is that He wants to go and make a beautiful place for believers to live throughout all eternity. How beautiful it will be! Streets of gold. Men kill one another for it here, but we will walk on it up there. Gates of jasper, walls of precious stones. The saints of all ages sitting upon the banks of the river of life!

Upon the throne, thank God, an ascended Jesus! The hope of Heaven.

"He was received up into heaven."—Mark 16:19.

THE SECOND COMING OF JESUS CHRIST

or

THE BIBLE DOCTRINE OF THE LORD'S RETURN

(Read: Hebrews 9:23-28)

"So Christ was once offered to bear the sins of many; and unto them that look for him shall he appear the second time without sin unto salvation."—Heb. 9:28.

   I. The Manner of His Coming

  II. The Mystery of His Coming

 III. The Motivation of His Coming

 IV. The Miracle of His Coming

  V. The Man of the Second Coming

 VI. The Message of His Coming

VII. The Millennium of His Coming

Road at the foot of the Mount of Olives

Looking toward Jerusalem, where Jesus will return to reign at His Second Coming

9

The Second Coming of Jesus Christ

or
The Bible Doctrine of the Lord's Return

"So Christ was once offered to bear the sins of many; and unto them that look for him shall he appear the second time without sin unto salvation."—Heb. 9:28.

I would like to point out to you in this Scripture three tremendous appearings of Jesus Christ. They are not in the order in which you read, but I want to point out the chronological order.

In verse 26 we read, "...but now once in the end of the world hath he appeared to put away sin by the sacrifice of himself." That was the first appearing of Jesus when He died upon the cross of Calvary.

In verse 24 we read, "...now to appear in the presence of God for us." That is His appearing as our Advocate at God's right hand in the Glory.

We read of the third appearing in verse 28, which is our text, "So Christ was once offered to bear the sins of many; and unto them that look for him shall he appear the second time without sin unto salvation."

There are a number of reasons why I feel led to preach on the second coming of Jesus Christ.

Misunderstood

For one thing it is one of the most misunderstood doctrines in the Bible. I do not know of any doctrine in the Bible—the doctrine of blood atonement, the doctrine of the inspiration of the Bible, the doctrine of the virgin birth, the deity of Christ, the doctrine of the resurrection of Christ from the dead—about which there has been more confusion, more difference of opinion, more misunderstanding, than the doctrine of the second coming of Christ.

Jesus knew what would happen, for in Matthew 24:4 He said, "Take heed that no man deceive you." Jesus is talking about His second coming, when He will appear again the second time without sin unto salvation to all those who look for Him. So Jesus said, "Take heed that no man deceive you."

Not Emphasized Enough

Not only is it a misunderstood doctrine, but the doctrine of the second coming of Jesus Christ is one that is not emphasized as it ought to be. In spite of the fact that the holy Scriptures give great emphasis to it, the church, the ministry, has not given that emphasis that God has given to it. In fact, in the Old Testament, in II Samuel 19, I read of the great frustration and confusion that took place under the kingdom and reign of David, Israel's greatest king. Then there was the betrayal by Absalom of his own father in the kingdom. Frustration reigned everywhere. War, anarchy, civil disturbance and violence took place. Then someone in II Samuel 19:10 said, "...why speak ye not a word of bringing the king back?" David had left the city of Jerusalem and someone said, "Why don't we bring the king back? That would solve this frustration and disturbance and violence and war. That would bring back peace again." "...why speak ye not a word of bringing the king back?"

I say to you that that is what we need to be thinking about. I am not going to be foolish enough to believe that peace will be brought by a little handful of men meeting over in Paris or at the United Nations, or anywhere else. "...why speak ye not a word of bringing the king back?" It is the bringing back of Jesus Christ alone that will restore order to this old sinful world. It is not emphasized enough.

Not Expected

The second coming of Jesus Christ is not expected. In Matthew 24:44 where Jesus spoke of His coming back to earth again, He said, "Therefore be ye also ready: for in such an hour as ye think not the Son of man cometh." We are living in an hour in our country when people, Bible-believing people, are not expecting the Son of God to come back again.

We read in this same chapter where Jesus gives a parable and says, "...that evil servant shall say in his heart, My Lord delayeth his coming" (Matt. 24:48).

I say to you that there are churches and preachers and Christians by the thousands across America who have no thought of the coming of Jesus Christ. They are not talking about it. They are not thinking about it. They are not praying about it. They are not expecting Him to come. I preach to you on the Second Coming because it is not expected. I preach to you on the Second Coming because it is not believed.

A Physical Coming

I have heard preachers preach on certain things that they refer to as the second coming of Christ. I have heard them preach at a funeral of a person who had died and say, "This is the coming of the Lord." I have heard people say that Pentecost was the second coming of Jesus Christ. I have heard people say it is a spiritual coming. He comes often when He comes to meet with His people. No, the promised return of Christ is not a spiritual coming, as I will show you further in my message. It is a bodily coming, a visible coming, a literal coming, and a real coming.

Jesus is coming, is coming! He is coming back again literally and bodily.

Not Loved

I preach to you on the second coming of Christ because it

is a doctrine that is not loved as it ought to be loved. In II Timothy 4:8 Paul said, "Henceforth there is laid up for me a crown of righteousness, which the Lord, the righteous judge, shall give me at that day: and not to me only, but unto all them also that love his appearing." Not many people really love the reality of the literal, bodily coming of our Lord Jesus Christ back to earth again.

I preach to you on the Second Coming because it is a part of the preaching of the Word. In II Timothy 4:2 God says to preachers, "Preach the word." In the New Testament alone, 318 times God refers to the second coming of Jesus Christ.

You cannot preach the Word without preaching the Second Coming. You cannot preach the Old Testament without preaching the Second Coming. In figure, and shadow, and type, and person, and place, you see pictures in the Old Testament of the second appearing of our Lord Jesus Christ back to this world again.

A Preacher at Bob Jones University

I never shall forget the first sermon I ever heard on the second coming of Jesus Christ after I was saved. I was a freshman in Bob Jones College. I had not been saved very long when I was called to preach. There came a young man to the college who spoke one day on the second coming of Jesus Christ. He talked about the rapture of Christians. He talked about the resurrection of those who sleep in Jesus. He talked about the responsibility of the church in the light of the coming of the Lord.

I never shall forget how my heart was stirred. I thought, He may come today! He may come before this day is ended!

So when I went to my room that day, first of all I searched my own heart, I confessed my sins, I searched my soul because I wanted to be ready when Jesus came. Then I wrote down the names of unsaved people, and I spent several hours writing letters, enclosing tracts and begging people to be saved.

I say to you that the Lord is coming. Even this great church needs to be reminded that Jesus Christ is coming back again.

The last words of any great will or testament are so important. When you come to the last chapter of the Bible, Revelation 22, it is significant to me that the Lord Jesus makes one statement three times. In verses 7, 12, 20, Jesus says, "Behold, I come quickly." "Behold I come quickly, keep this word," He said. "Behold I come quickly, my reward is with me," He said. "Behold I come quickly"; and then John said, 'Even so, come Lord Jesus; I want you to come.'

I wonder, my friend, if you have ever said that—"Even so, come Lord Jesus"? Let me ask you, honestly, carefully, Would you like for Him to come today? Are you ready for Him to come? Are you expecting Jesus to return? There are two or three things that should be clarified about the doctrine of the Second Coming.

Second Coming in Two Parts

Speaking of the coming of the Lord, the Bible sometimes speaks in the same passage of two great things about His second coming. There is what is called the rapture at His coming, then the revelation at His coming. He is coming to take the people of God with Him, then He is coming back with those people of God. His coming for His people is called the rapture. The word *rapture* is not found in the Bible, but *rapture* means to be "caught up." And that expression is found in the Bible.

In I Thessalonians 4:17 we read, "Then we which are alive and remain shall be caught up together with them in the clouds, to meet the Lord in the air: and so shall we ever be with the Lord."

Then after seven years He is coming again. He is not

coming this time for His people, but He is coming with His saints in the clouds of Glory. This is called the revelation. There is a distinction made between the rapture and the revelation.

Paul speaks of the revelation in I Thessalonians 2:13: "...at the coming of our Lord Jesus Christ with all his saints." Then He will rule and reign upon the earth for a thousand years.

I want to give you seven great truths about the second coming of the Lord Jesus Christ.

I. THE MANNER OF HIS COMING

How is He coming? What will it be like when He comes again? This is described in Acts 1, on the occasion of His ascension. We read four times in this chapter, "He was taken up." "He was taken up." "He was taken up." "He was taken up." In Acts 1:10,11 we read that when He went up, two men dressed in white apparel came down. They were men from Heaven, angelic messengers. They came down as He went up. These men gave a message to the church: "Ye men of Galilee, why stand ye gazing up into heaven? this same Jesus, which is taken up from you into heaven, shall so come in like manner as ye have seen him go into heaven."

How can we know how Christ will come back again? Two angels were sent from the throne of God to tell us that He would come back just exactly like He went away. "This same Jesus...shall so come in like manner as ye have seen him go...." If I want to know how He is coming back, then I will examine how He went away. How did He go away?

Suddenly

He went away suddenly. For forty days and nights He appeared to the believers between the resurrection and the ascension, sometimes to as few as one, like Mary at the grave; sometimes to as many as five hundred at one time.

After the resurrection and before the ascension, Jesus appeared only to believers. At the end of these forty days He walks near the Mount of Olives. I wish I had time to show you how He is coming back to the same place where He went up that day—back to the Mount of Olives, near the little town of Bethany. All of a sudden He stretches out His nail-pierced hands, the heavens light up with the glory of God, it seems an invisible stairway reaches down from Heaven to the rocks of earth, and Jesus begins to climb that stairway back into the presence of God. To the amazement of the disciples, He went away. Suddenly He went away.

Listen, He is coming back suddenly. He said, "Behold, I come quickly." Suddenly He is coming back. He said in Matthew 24:27, "For as the lightning cometh out of the east, and shineth even unto the west; so shall also the coming of the Son of man be." Jesus said like a flash of lightning. Paul said like the twinkling of an eye. Suddenly He went away, suddenly He will come back.

How is He coming back? Like He went away—suddenly.

Bodily

How is He coming back? He is coming back like He went away and He went away bodily. Don't tell me the second coming of Jesus is merely a spiritual truth. Thank God, it is a glorious reality. For when Jesus went away, He went away in a body. Let me remind you that it was a body that could take food; it was a body that could be seen; it was a body that could be touched; it was a body out of which He spake; it was a body out of which He felt and saw.

He went away in a body and He will come again in a body. Going away in a body He demonstrated how He would come back. He went away visibly, bodily, literally and He will come back the same way.

In Luke 24:39 before He went away, He said, "Behold my hands and my feet, that it is I myself: handle me, and see; for a spirit hath not flesh and bones, as ye see me have."

He said, "I am not just a ghost; I am not a phantom; I am not merely a spirit; I am a real body." That is the way He went away and thank God, that is the way He is coming back. The Bible says, "This same Jesus...." That is the One I want. I want the One who one day came from Heaven's highest pedestal to earth's lowest point. I want the One, thank God, who came through the body of a virgin woman. I want the One who walked in a human body. I want the One, thank God, who went about doing good. I want the same One, thank God, who was baptized in the River Jordan. I want the same One, thank God, who died upon a cross, was robed in blood and crowned with thorns.

That is the Jesus I want. That is the Jesus the Bible says who is coming back. This same Jesus. How did He go away? He went away bodily; He will come back bodily.

In Presence of His Own

How did He go away? He went away in the presence of His own only. When He went up that day, not one sinner saw Him. Not one unconverted person saw Jesus after He hung on that cross, robed in blood and crowned with thorns. The next time they see Him, they will see Him coming in power and great glory, not as a Lamb slain, but as a Lion of the tribe of Judah. That day He went up in the presence of His own.

In the first three verses of John 14 Jesus said, "Let not your heart be troubled: ye believe in God, believe also in me. In my Father's house are many mansions: if it were not so, I would have told you. I go to prepare a place for you. And if I go and prepare a place for you, I will come again, and receive you unto myself; that where I am, there ye may be also."

He is coming for saved people. When He comes, only the saved will be caught away.

I read a story some time ago about a father and daughter who loved the water, and loved swimming. One day off the coast of New Jersey, the father and daughter were swimming in the Atlantic Ocean. Before they had realized it, they had drifted far from shore. The waves were becoming higher and the winds stronger. Suddenly they realized they were in danger.

The story is that the father said to the daughter, "Now, daughter, you are a good swimmer. You can float on your back all day long. You do not have a thing to worry about. Turn over on your back and float and I will be back."

The father swam to shore with great difficulty. Hours wore on. He got help and went out in the boat and began to look. Sure enough, someone said, "Look, there is a body floating in the water." They wondered if she had drowned or if she was safe. They found her floating on her back, looking up at the blue sky, as relaxed as she could be after hours in the water. They were surprised she seemed so well, not alarmed and not afraid. They said to her, "You are so relaxed."

She said, "Why shouldn't I be? My father who loves me said he was going away for a little while but he was coming back."

When I think of the coming of Jesus, I remember He said, "I am going away but I will be back. I will be back."

Thank God, He is coming back. "Even so come, Lord Jesus."

"For yet a little while, and he that shall come will come and will not tarry."—Heb. 10:37.

"...and unto them that look for him shall he appear the second time without sin unto salvation."—Heb. 9:28.

II. THE MYSTERY OF HIS COMING

Let us go on to another great part of the second coming of Jesus Christ. Not only is there the manner of His coming but the mystery of His coming. I do not mean it is something you cannot understand. When I refer to mystery, I mean what the Bible means. A mystery in the Bible is something heretofore unexplained but now made clear.

That is what Paul meant when he said the Gospel was a mystery. It was never clearly understood until Christ came and grace came and took the place of law. But the Bible says there is a mystery about the coming of the Lord.

Now Paul mentioned it in I Corinthians 15:51,52, "Behold, I shew you a mystery; We shall not all sleep, but we shall all be changed, In a moment, in the twinkling of an eye, at the last trump: for the trumpet shall sound, and the dead shall be raised incorruptible, and we shall be changed." Notice Paul said in connection with the coming of Christ, "I shew you a mystery; We shall not all sleep."

Now, what is this mystery? It is a fourfold mystery and I would like to deal with these four mysteries.

Some People Will Never Die

First, it is the mystery that some will never die. We use the expression, "As sure as death and taxes." Now taxes are pretty sure, but death is not near as certain. This Bible teaches that a generation of Christians are never going to die. Generation after generation of Christians have lived with the hope that they may never die. Christ may come before I die. Paul said, "Behold I shew you a mystery; We shall not all sleep, but we shall all be changed." I live with the hope that Jesus will come in my lifetime. I am not a date-setter. I do not spend my time looking for signs of the coming of the Saviour, but I hope He will come in my lifetime. And I can easily believe that Christ will come before I go to be with Him.

The grave holds no fear for me. The grave holds no fear for a Christian, but our hope is the coming of the Lord, and how important that is. When you come right down to it, there is only one way anyone is going to get to Heaven and that is through the second coming of Jesus Christ. If you die before He comes, that old body goes back to dust. The spirit alone is "absent from the body, and present with the Lord." When the Lord comes, He brings that body incorruptible out of that grave, clothed in immortality, and soul and spirit are united, and the man who is a trinity in all of His fulness then will be in Heaven with the Lord. "Behold, I shew you a mystery; We shall not all sleep."

Translation of the Living

There is a second wonderful mystery, the mystery of the translation of the living. "We shall not all sleep, but we shall all be changed." When you are saved, your body is not saved. When you are saved, your spirit is saved, your soul is saved, but your body doesn't get converted when the Lord comes into your heart. Your body will be converted when the Lord comes.

At the translation—as the old song says,

> "This robe of flesh I'll drop and rise
> To seize the everlasting prize."

If your body were converted, you would never lose your teeth. If your body were regenerated, your hair would never turn gray. If your body were regenerated, you would never become stoop-shouldered. If your body were regenerated, you would never wear glasses. Our bodies are not born again when we are, but they shall be changed.

Thank God, I'll have a body like His! A body that knows no pain, one that experiences no fatigue, and holds no unsatisfied hunger, with every desire realized, I will have a body like unto His body.

There are pictures of this translation throughout the Bible. I like to read in Genesis about a man named Enoch. One day Enoch walked with God and God said, "Enoch, it is getting late; you had better go home."

Enoch said, "Lord, it's so good to walk with You; I have enjoyed this fellowship so much; I don't want to go back home. You will go back into Heaven—I just wish I could stay with You."

Maybe the Lord said, "All right, Enoch. You have such a holy desire, such a burning aspiration to be with Me." And we read this statement, "And Enoch walked with God: and he was not for God took him" (Gen. 5:24). Just like Enoch was translated without dying, so will the living Christians be when Jesus comes.

I read of Elijah (God bless his sainted memory), old, shaggy Elijah, the prophet of God who closed the heavens until it did not rain and opened them until a flood came. Old Elijah one day saw the heavens open and saw the chariot of God come down and Elijah went to Heaven without dying.

I have heard people say, "Wouldn't it be wonderful to be like old Lazarus, to get raised from the dead." I don't know whether I would want that or not. I really don't. I thank God for the story and for the experience and the power and the miracle, but I don't know if I want that or not. I think once I go, I want to stay until the Lord comes. Lazarus died, and the Lord raised him. I don't know how long he lived, but a few years later his old heart began to slow down and his body grew weak and he died again. I think once is enough!

I thank God that I have something better than Lazarus had. He had to die twice. I know if the Lord tarries, I will only have to die one time. Then when He comes, there will be the resurrection of the dead, the translation of the living.

Time

Now, notice, there is in the mystery of His coming, the mystery of time. No one knows when the Lord is coming. No one has any right to set a date. Now I deal with the mystery of time and iniquity.

Listen, no one knows when the Lord is coming. His coming is imminent. I mean by that that He could come right now. Though His coming is certain, the time is unknown.

Jesus made some strange statements along this line. See Matthew 24:36: "But of that day and hour knoweth no man." Read all the signs you want to, but you are not going to know when the Lord is coming. "But of that day and hour knoweth no man, no, not the angels of heaven, but my Father only." Jesus said only His Father knows when He is coming back. Listen to it again: "Watch therefore: for ye know not what hour your Lord doth come." Listen to it again: "Watch therefore, for ye know neither the day nor the hour wherein the Son of man cometh" (Matt. 24:42).

He told the parable of the ten virgins. Five were wise, five were foolish; five were saved and asleep, five were lost and asleep. The Lord came, and none of them were prepared. Not even the saved were watching for the coming of the Lord. He said, "Watch therefore, for ye know neither the day nor the hour wherein the Son of man cometh" (Matt. 25:13).

Now listen, some of the most tragic things that have ever happened have happened because some people have not believed what Jesus said about the time of His coming. You cannot know.

People say, "Aren't there signs?" Yes, there will be signs later, but listen, these signs will not point to the rapture; they will point to the revelation. They do not point to the coming *for* His church; they will point to His coming *with* the church. I do not believe there are signs in the Bible that point to the rapture alone. Not to the rapture, but to the revelation.

There was a man years ago in New York State named William Miller, a good man, no doubt, in many ways. He had a Bible and a Cruden's concordance.. He studied. He got in the book of Daniel. He got mixed up and confused and was not able to rightly divide the Word of truth. William Miller set a date. In 1831 he said that on a certain day about twelve years later in 1843, the Lord would come.

Some say he had folks dressed in white get on the highest building, barn or haystack they could get on.

That day came and passed, but Jesus did not come. The reason He didn't is that Jesus said, "No man knoweth the hour." If one says Jesus is coming a certain day in 1968, I know He won't come on that day because Jesus said no one knows the day nor hour. Miller got mixed up. The Lord didn't come. So William Miller said, "What I should have said is that He will enter the heavenly sanctuary and start His intercessory work."

From that has sprung some false religions that are not true to the Bible. They have started a lot of confusion about the second coming of Jesus Christ.

Charles Taze Russell set a date in 1914. He said, "The Lord is coming." In 1914 we were in a war that took the lives of millions of people, but Jesus did not come. Date-setters, sign-readers, God says, "No man knows the day nor hour." God has no place for these people in the Bible.

Iniquity

Paul in II Thessalonians 2:7 says, "For the mystery of iniquity doth already work: only he who now letteth [hinder-eth] will let." (*Letteth* is an old English translation of the word *hinder*.) That is, someone will hinder someone's hindering of the mystery of iniquity.

The Antichrist—Someone is holding him back. Who? The Holy Spirit of God. He who now hindereth will be taken out of the way. That is the Holy Spirit. He will be removed, in the sense of dwelling in Christians and their influence on affairs, when the church is taken up. That is the Second Coming. "And then shall that Wicked be revealed, whom the Lord shall consume with the spirit of his mouth, and shall destroy with the brightness of his coming."

This refers to the Antichrist. God's holy Word says that the Antichrist, who will talk about peace and whose words will be as smooth butter, cannot come until the Holy Spirit is taken out of the way. The Holy Spirit cannot leave, thank God, until I leave. He cannot go until I go. He will not leave until you leave, and He will leave with His restraining influence through Christians when the church is raptured up, when the Lord Jesus shall come again. That may take place at any time.

I wonder, my friend, are you ready for His coming? It is either Christ or Antichrist. Which is it for you? It is either reign with Him or ruin with the Devil. Which shall it be for you?

"And unto them that look for him shall he appear the second time without sin unto salvation."—Heb. 9:28.

III. THE MOTIVATION OF HIS COMING

In I John 3:1-3 we read,

"Behold, what manner of love the Father hath bestowed upon us, that we should be called the sons of God; therefore the world knoweth us not, because it knew him not. Beloved, now are we the sons of God, and it doth not yet appear what we shall be: but we know that, when he shall appear, we shall be like him; for we shall see him as he is. And every man that hath this hope in him purifieth himself, even as he is pure."

I would like now to talk about the motivation of His coming. In these verses it is talking about the motivation in the lives of people concerning the second coming of Jesus Christ.

Holy Living

So the first thing about the Second Coming, a real deep belief and conviction that the Lord is coming, is that it should motivate a Christian to holy living. The Scripture says, "...every man that hath this hope in him purifieth himself, even as he is pure." So the second coming of Christ should motivate Christians to holy, clean, pure living before the Lord.

I read an interesting story the other day about a visitor who came to a school. The visitor said, "We want to see which child in this school can keep his desk the cleanest. I am not going to tell you when I will be back but I will be back to make an inspection and see who has the cleanest desk."

The story is that one little girl said, "I am going to have the cleanest desk when the inspector comes back. I am going to have the cleanest desk of all."

Some said, "We don't know how you can have the cleanest desk. Your desk is usually the most untidy and the most disheveled and the most out of order."

She said, "Well then, I am going to clean it every week of the world."

They said, "Suppose the inspector came back just before you cleaned it, and it hadn't been cleaned in a week? Then you would not have the cleanest desk."

She said, "Well, then I will clean it every morning."

They said, "Suppose he comes in the late afternoon and all day long you have been using it, then your desk wouldn't be the cleanest."

The little girl thought for a moment, then said, "I will tell you what I am going to do. I am going to keep it clean all the time; then it won't matter when he comes."

This ought to be the attitude of every child of God. "... every man that hath this hope in him purifieth himself, even as he is pure."

The motivation of the second coming of Jesus Christ is toward purity of life. In I John 2:28 we read, "And now, little children, abide in him; that, when he shall appear, we may have confidence, and not be ashamed before him at his coming." So the Second Coming motivates to holy living.

Prayer

In the second place, it motivates us to prayer. In Mark 13:33 Jesus said, "Take heed, watch and pray: for ye know not when the time is." Now, I do not understand the depth of this wonderful statement by Jesus Christ, "Take heed, watch and pray: for ye know not when the time is." But it has to do with the second coming of Jesus Christ. In other words, Jesus is saying here, 'If you do not know when I am coming, then the thing for you to do is be in the spirit of prayer all the time. Take ye heed, watch and pray: for ye know not when the time is.'

I heard of a young girl who went away to college years ago. Some students said to her the first night she was at school, "The girls have a prayer meeting tonight down the hall." The girl was listening to popular music on her radio and she said, "I am not going to prayer meeting." She lay down on her bed in her dormitory room and listened to her radio. She began to think. She thought of the girls down the hall just like herself, kneeling in prayer. She thought of the coming of the Lord. She thought, Suppose the Lord should come with a prayer meeting going on a few feet away from me and my mind was occupied with something else.

It is said that she ran out of her room, down to where the girls were praying, pushed herself in the midst and began to sob and pray, "O God, help me to be ready for the coming of the Lord!"

So the second coming of Jesus Christ is motivation to prayer.

Separation

This Bible plainly teaches that when the Lord comes, God's people are to be living a separated life, a dedicated life. Let me read that to you out of the Word of God, in Titus 2:11-14:

"For the grace of God that bringeth salvation hath appeared to all men, Teaching us that, denying ungodliness and worldly lusts, we should live soberly, righteously, and godly, in this present world; Looking for that blessed hope, and the glorious appearing of the great God and our Saviour

*Jesus Christ; Who gave himself for us, that he might re-
deem us from all iniquity, and purify unto himself a peculiar people, zealous of good works."*

Notice what it says. We are to be "looking for that
blessed hope. and the glorious appearing of the great God
and our Saviour Jesus Christ." Why? Because this Bible
teaches us that denying ungodliness and worldly desires, we
should live soberly, righteously and godly in this present
age as we are looking for the coming of Jesus Christ.

I ran across some beautiful lines of poetry the other day
entitled "Quite Suddenly":

Quite suddenly—it may be at the turning of a lane,
Where I stand to watch a skylark soar from out the swelling grain,
That the trump of God shall thrill me, with its call so loud and clear,
And I'm called away to meet Him, whom of all I hold most dear.

Quite suddenly—it may be as I tread the busy street,
Strong to endure life's stress and strain, its every call to meet,
That through the roar of traffic, a trumpet, silvery clear,
Shall stir my startled senses, and proclaim His coming near.

Quite suddenly—it may be as I lie in dreamless sleep—
God's gift to many a sorrowing heart, with no more tears to weep—
That a call shall break my slumber, and a voice sound in my ear,
"Rise up, My love, and come away, behold the Bridegroom's here!"

So the second coming of Jesus Christ is a motivation to
separation.

Soul Winning

I feel with all my heart that every one of us need a quick-
ening, a stirring, a new consciousness, a new dedication to
this matter of soul winning. If Satan fights anything in the
work of God, he fights to keep people from winning lost
souls.

It is said that I Thessalonians deals with the rapture of
the church or the coming of Christ for His saints. Second

Thessalonians deals principally with the coming of Christ with His saints. But notice a peculiar, yet wonderful thing about First Thessalonians. Every single chapter, all five chapters, end with a special message about the coming of Jesus Christ. Chapter two of I Thessalonians ends with the message about the coming of the Lord and soul winning. For Paul says, "For what is our hope, or joy, or crown of rejoicing? Are not even ye in the presence of our Lord Jesus Christ at his coming" (vs. 19). He said, "When the Lord comes, what will be my crown in that hour? When the Lord comes, what will be my rejoicing when I meet Him?" He said, "Are not even ye, you people I have won, you who have been saved under my ministry?"

It will be an embarassing moment for a Christian who has never won a single soul to Jesus Christ, who stands before the Lord empty-handed at His coming, with no reward for soul winning. The second coming of Jesus Christ is a motivation for soul winning.

I know beyond any shadow of doubt that when the Lord comes, whether it be in this generation or the next or the next—no matter when it is, He is going to find a group of Christians who are saved and who will be caught away to meet Him in the air. When the Lord comes, regardless of when it will be, He will find loved ones who are lost, or friends and neighbors, whom you have made no effort to win. The second coming of Jesus Christ ought to motivate people to win lost souls.

I mentioned to you in the first part of my message about the first sermon I ever heard on the second coming of Christ after I was saved. I was a country boy, just reaching the age of twenty. I was in my freshman year at the Bob Jones College in Cleveland, Tennessee. As I heard that man, he looked as if he were reaching up into the stars while he preached. Oh, what oratory! What power of God! What a thrilling description of the coming of Christ! It changed my life. There was a new power that swept over me. There was a new compassion that came into my heart. I went to my room to write and send tracts. I went out on the street corners to witness, to win someone to Christ. Motivation, motivation for soul winning is the second coming of Jesus Christ.

Steadfast Living and Waiting

In the fifth place, it is also a motivation for patient waiting and steadfast living. James mentioned this, in James 5:7,8: "Be patient therefore, brethren, unto the coming of the Lord...." Oh, what could be said about it! What I could say to my own heart about it! "Be patient therefore, brethren, unto the coming of the Lord."

For one thing, if you study carefully that chapter in James, you will find that he mentions people who had been wronged. He mentioned, "Some of you rich people have wronged people who work for you. You didn't pay them what you ought to have paid." And he says to the workmen, 'You just wait. Be patient therefore, brethren, unto the coming of the Lord. You don't have to make it right. The Lord will make it right. Vengeance is mine, I will repay, saith the Lord. Be patient therefore, brethren, unto the coming of the Lord.'

He will show who is right and who is wrong. So he says to Christians who have been wronged, "Be patient therefore, brethren, unto the coming of the Lord." He also said, "Be ye also patient; stablish your hearts: for the coming of the Lord draweth nigh." Then in James 5:9 he says, "...the judge standeth before the door."

You know 1900 years ago James wrote this book and said, "He is standing at the door. I am expecting Him any minute. The Lord is coming." The expected thing that ought to be in the heart of every Christian is that the coming of the Lord is imminent. Every shadow may be His shadow. Every knock may be His knock. Every trumpet may be His trumpet. Every shout may be His shout. The coming of the

Lord! "Be ye patient, stablish your hearts: for the coming of the Lord draweth nigh."

A friend of mine years ago told me a sweet and wonderful story. I am sure that it is true. He said one Saturday afternoon, down in the southland where he and I were raised, he overheard a fine-looking colored man and a fine-looking, clean-faced colored boy. They had come to town like country people always did down South on Saturday afternoon.

This colored man said to this little boy, his little son, "Now, Son, I am going across the street, up those stairs, in that office. You wait right here on this corner, in front of this store, and I will be back in a moment."

The little boy stood there. The father walked across the street, into the office. The little colored boy continued to stand. This man who told me the story said just then, it began to get black, and there began the thunder and the flash of lightning. Then all of a sudden, quicker than you could tell it, it seems the heavens became a torrent of rain and it began to pour.

The little boy stood on the street and he was becoming drenched with the rain. People were scurrying here and there to seek shelter. Someone said, "Come in here, little boy."

The little boy said, "No, my daddy said wait right here; he would be back in a little while. I can't come in there."

Someone else came along, took him by the shoulders and said, "Little boy, come in here out of the storm."

He said, "No, I am waiting for my daddy to come."

After a short time the storm subsided. The colored man came down from the office, down the stairs and across the street. He saw his little boy dripping wet. The little boy said, "Daddy, I wanted to be right where you told me to be when you came back."

Let me tell you, my friend, God has a place He wants you to be. He has a standard of Christian living He wants you to measure up to when He comes back. The second coming of Jesus Christ is the motivation of patient, steadfast living for the Son of God.

"And unto them that look for him shall he appear the second time without sin unto salvation."—Heb. 9:28.

IV. THE MIRACLE OF HIS COMING

I want you to notice the miracle of His coming. It is as I have said before, there are people who want to take away the reality of His coming. They want to spiritualize it. I want you to notice that everything about Jesus is a miracle.

Take His virgin birth. Being born without an earthly father was a miracle, my friends.

Take His spotless life. He lived without sin. He could say, "Who convinces me of sin?" That was a miracle, my friends.

Take His death upon a bloody cross, planned before the foundation of the world, ordained of God before a star was ever hung. Take His death, where He laid down His life, with no man taking it from Him. That was a miracle, my friends.

Take His resurrection from that stoney tomb, after being bound in the graveclothes three days and three nights. That was a miracle, my friends.

Take His ascension from the Mount of Olives that day back into Glory. That was a miracle, my friends.

Jesus is coming again. He will split the sky and blow the trumpet in the clouds and claim His own. It will be a miracle, the miracle of His coming.

The Miracle of the Resurrection

There are many miracles involved in the Second Coming. There is the miracle of resurrection. For when He comes, Jesus said, "...Marvel not at this, for the hour is coming, in the which all that are in the graves shall hear his voice, and shall come forth; they that have done good, unto the resurrection of life; and they that have done evil, unto the resurrection of damnation" (John 5:28,29). Jesus is coming and when He comes there is going to be a resurrection. What a sweet truth to saved people, but what an awful truth to unsaved people! The unsaved shall be raised for judgment. The saved shall be raised to live with Jesus forevermore.

I can hardly wait for that glorious hour. It is going to be a wonderful day when the Lord comes and out of the graves come those we love who sleep in Jesus. Mothers and dads, children we have lost for a while, brothers and sisters, husbands and wives, will rise to the most glorious reunion the world has ever known. They will step out of those tombs when the Lord comes and the resurrection takes place. The miracle of resurrection.

The Miracle of a New Body

Paul constantly spoke of the miracle of a new body. He needed one. The one He had was worn out and beaten almost to shreds. In Philippians 3:20, 21 Jesus said, "For our conversation [citizenship] is in heaven: from whence also we look for the Saviour, the Lord Jesus Christ: Who shall change our vile body, that it may be fashioned like unto his glorious body, according to the working whereby he is able even to subdue all things unto himself."

I like that! That verse not only teaches I am going to be *with* Him; it teaches I am going to be *like* Him! Like Him! We will have a body like Jesus'. Talk about space! I am going to be an astronaut. I will jump from one star to another. I am going to eat breakfast on the moon and lunch on Mars. Talk about space! That body can walk through doors. It knows no limitation. It is a body like unto His. It is the miracle of the new body.

The Miracle of the Rapture

Let me say to you, that miracle of the rapture is going to take place. You can believe it or not believe it. Just think of the doctrine: it is a reality that the Lord is going to come and like a mighty drawing magnetism He is going to draw out of this world all those who belong to Him. Jesus spoke of it in Luke 17: "...two men in one bed; the one shall be taken, and the other shall be left. Two women shall be grinding together; the one shall be taken, and the other left. Two men shall be in the field; the one shall be taken, and the other left." There you read it. Three times it says, "one shall be taken, the other left." That is the miracle of the rapture.

My friend, you are on this side or the other—the one who will be taken or the one who will be left. The unsaved people will be left. That is the miracle of the rapture.

The Miracle of Peace

When I contemplate how little peace there is in this world, and how much war there has been in my lifetime of a half century or so, it is almost unbelievable. The two greatest wars the world has ever known have taken place in my lifetime and in the lifetime of most of you. At this moment the fires of war burn on many continents and on many battlefields.

It is said that in World War I more people were killed than in all the wars fought before. In World War II there were more people killed than in all the wars of all history, since time began. Only God knows what it will be like if there is another one.

Do you know that this nation of ours has the potential to destroy millions of people at one time? Do you know that one airplane can carry power and weapons to blot out a city like New York or Moscow? I pray God this generation may never have another war.

On that beautiful night when the shepherds kept their flocks on the moonlit fields, the angels came to speak and they said, "Glory to God in the highest, and on earth, peace, good will toward men" (Luke 2:14). They announced that night the coming of the Prince of Peace. Thirty-three years later they nailed Him to a cross and cried, "Crucify Him." For two thousand years this world has known nothing but blood and destruction.

But, thank God, He is going to come again. After He comes, this world will know a millennium of peace. I read in Isaiah 9:6, "For unto us a child is born, unto us a son is given: and the government shall be upon his shoulder: and his name shall be called Wonderful, Counsellor, The mighty God, the everlasting Father, the Prince of Peace. Of the increase of his government and peace there shall be no end ...."

I will tell you something you already know: there will never be peace on this earth until Jesus Christ, the Prince of Peace, comes to reign, whose right it is and whose right alone it is to reign. The miracle of His coming! The miracle of the resurrection! The miracle of a new body! The miracle of the rapture! The miracle of peace!

"And unto them that look for him shall he appear the second time without sin unto salvation."—Heb. 9:28.

V. THE MAN OF THE SECOND COMING

I would like to have time to talk about the Man of the Second Coming. I do not want you to think of just a doctrine; I do not want you to think of just a hope; I do not want you to have just a dream; but I want you to think of it as a reality. The Bible says, "This same Jesus" (Acts 1:11). A Person is coming, a Person I have longed to see for thirty-three years. A Person is coming.

When the states of Italy were united by a great man by the name of Garibaldi, it is said that they would write on the sidewalks at night, "Garibaldi is coming!" I stood in Rome on a hill and saw the beautiful bronze statue of that liberator. They called Garibaldi the Liberator. At night they would whisper on the streets, "Garibaldi is coming! Garibaldi is coming!"

I feel tonight from the depths of my ransomed soul, Jesus is coming! Jesus is coming! The Man of the Second Coming. The same Jesus who died and arose. The same One who saves and keeps. That same Jesus is coming—the Lord Himself. First Thessalonians 4:16 says "the Lord Himself" is coming.

"And unto them that look for him shall he appear the second time without sin unto salvation."—Heb. 9:28.

VI. THE MESSAGE OF HIS COMING

Notice with me the message of His coming. What does it mean?

To the Church

There is first the message to the church. In Luke 19:13 Jesus said, "Occupy till I come." The message is that the ministry of the church is to send the blessed gospel message to the ends of the earth. "Occupy till I come." That means let yourself be known. It means be heard from. It means peddle your wares. It means take forth what you have. It means use your talent. "Occupy till I come."

To the Jews

I wish I had the time to talk about the message to the Jew, that man in his blindness who does not recognize Jesus as the Messiah, that man in his nationalistic movement who thinks all he has to do is go back to Israel, the promised land, and peace will come. But he goes back in darkness and unbelief and wars. The book of Zechariah deals with that. I read where one day the Jew shall see Him and say to Him, "What are these wounds in thine hands?" Jesus will answer, "Those with which I was wounded in the house of my friends" (Zech. 13:6). They shall mourn for Him whom they pierced. There is a message to the Jews.

To the World

There is a message to the world. Mark it down: when

Jesus comes, this world is going to be judged. I just wish that everyone in this world could hear the word of Jesus about His coming and its relationship to this world. In Matthew 25, Jesus Himself is speaking:

"When the Son of man shall come in his glory, and all the holy angels with him, then shall he sit upon the throne of his glory: And before him shall be gathered all nations: and he shall separate them one from another, as a shepherd divideth his sheep from the goats: And he shall set the sheep on his right hand, but the goats on the left. Then shall the King say unto them on his right hand, Come, ye blessed of my Father, inherit the kingdom prepared for you from the foundation of the world."

Two things here He says to the saved. He says, "Come ye blessed of my Father, inherit the kingdom prepared for you from the foundation of the world." Jesus will say unto them in that day, "These shall go away into everlasting punishment: but the righteous unto life eternal." There is going to be a division, my friends. The Lord is going to divide the sheep from the goats.

Someone tried to win a judge one time in Atlanta, Georgia. One said to him, "I understand you and your wife are going to separate."

The judge said, "Why, that's a lie. My wife and I have lived together some forty-odd years. We have no plans to separate."

The friend said to the judge, "It is true you are going to be separated."

The judge asked, "What do you mean?"

"Well, your wife is a Christian and you are unsaved. When the Lord comes, she is going to be taken and you are going to be left. You are going to be judged."

He said, "Well, that may be true." That smote his heart with conviction. A message to the world.

To the Sinner

There is the message to the sinner. When Jesus comes it is then too late to prepare for the rapture. Oh, may God speak to the heart of any in reach of this message who are lost. May you realize that when Jesus comes, you will be left behind. Paul wrote the greatest chapter on the subject of the resurrection, the fifteenth chapter of I Corinthians. In that chapter there are five whole systems of truths that have to do with the resurrection of Jesus Christ that Paul develops, explains and dwells on. But when he comes to the close of the sixteenth chapter of I Corinthians he says, "If any man loves not the Lord Jesus Christ, let him be Anathema Maranatha." Maranatha means "at the coming of the Lord." Anathema means "accursed, judged, destroyed." Paul said, "If any man love not the Saviour, let him be cursed at the coming of the Lord." That is what is going to happen to unsaved people who are left behind. A message to the sinner.

Years ago there was an event in India called "Siege of Lucknow." It is said that there was a group of English soldiers and officials in a fort which was being sieged by Indian rebels. These few men were about to be overcome. They said, "There is no way out." So they began to scatter and look for a way of escape. It is said that one man wandered off by himself while all the others found a way out through a tunnel under the cellar. Down through the cellar they went, through the tunnel hundreds of yards up out in the woodlands and to safety.

It is said that when this one man discovered all companions gone and finding no way of escape, he began to scream, "I am left behind! I am left behind!" After some hours he found that escape and he too went out through it and hours later joined his companions. It is said that in those few hours his hair, black as a raven's wing, turned white as the winter's snow. For days he talked with a mumbling of speech that was hardly discernible. His mind would come and go. When this happened he would scream, "Left behind! Left behind!"

Let me tell you, my friends, you may mock the Son of God; you may laugh at Christians; you may mock at the preaching of the old-fashioned Word of God; but wait until the hour comes when the true church is removed, when there is no more Gospel preached, no more songs sung, no more praying, no more weeping over your soul—wait until that fact grips your heart: Christ has come and I am left behind. You say, "Well, people are going to be saved after the Lord comes." That is true. Revelation speaks of a great host which no man can number who come out of the tribulation and make their robes white with the blood of the Lamb. But let me tell you, I fear it won't be you. I firmly believe that it will be people that have never heard the Gospel. I believe the man or woman who hears the Gospel and has had a chance to be saved and won't be saved, will not likely be saved after the Lord comes.

A poem says:

> In the glow of early morning
> In the solemn hush of night;
> Down from Heaven's open portals,
> Steals a messenger of light.
> Whisp'ring sweetly to my spirit,
> While the hosts of Heaven sing,
> 'Tis the wondrous, thrilling story,
> Christ is coming—Christ my King.
>
> Oft methinks I hear His footsteps,
> Stealing down the paths of time,
> And the future dark with shadows,
> Brightens with this Hope sublime;
> Sound the soul-inspiring anthem,
> Angel hosts, your harps attune;
> Earth's long night is almost over,
> Christ is coming—coming soon.

"And unto them that look for him shall he appear the second time without sin unto salvation."—Heb. 9:28.

VII. THE MILLENNIUM OF HIS COMING

I close by saying that there is the millennium of His coming. Oh, I wish I could describe it, the millennium of His coming. The word *millennium* is not found in the Bible, just like the word *rapture* is not found in the Bible. But *millennium* is a compound word of two Latin words which mean a thousand years, and that is found in the Bible. In Revelation 20:1-7 six times the Lord mentions a "thousand years." During those thousand years the Lord will reign. The Bible says the desert shall blossom like a rose. The knowledge of the Lord shall cover the earth as the waters cover the sea. The lamb and the lion shall lie down together. Roses will be without thorns. The deserts shall be watered. And when the Lord comes, it will be an age of beauty, the like of which the world has never known before. The millennium of His coming!

During the millennium Satan will be bound. There will be no more war. Thank God, there will be no disease, no curse, no violence, no fear, no sorrow, for the Lord will be here. The Bible says when He reigns we are going to reign with Him. Thank God for the glorious hope of the coming of the Lord!

In closing, I want to tell you a beautiful true story that I heard Edgerton Long tell a good many years ago. Edgerton Long was a missionary. He knew for a fact of a little community where the old two-story frame school building where children went was a veritable fire trap. The community talked about it, but no new school had been built. A fireman in that community had a little girl in the school. Often he would call his little girl, take her up on his lap, put his arms around her and say, "Now darling, your daddy is a fireman. It is my business, my training, to rescue people when buildings catch on fire. Someday the old school may catch on fire and if it does, there will be confusion. People will run for the door and many will not escape. If the building ever does catch on fire, I want to tell you what to do. When the big fire bell rings at the school, I want you to sit in your seat. I know where it is. Don't move if the fire bell rings because I am coming for you."

Then one day, sure enough, the fire alarm sounded. The men with their boots and fire equipment jumped on the truck. It went hustling through the streets of the little community. Someone said, "Where are we going? Where is the fire?" They answered, "The school building is burning."

When they reached the building, the smoke was coming from the windows. It is said that the stairways were covered with bodies choking and dying. When they put the big ladders against the buildings, the big old fireman climbed a ladder, broke through the windows and over across the room at the door lay bodies piled one on top of the other.

But sitting there with her little head bowed, at her desk, was the little girl. The big man swept the little girl up in his arms and back down the ladder he went.

Let me tell you, my friends, this old Bible tells me that someday this earth will melt with fervent heat. The fire is coming. One of these days God will ring the judgment bell telling that this earth is to be destroyed.

Thank God, there is One coming—the Rock of Ages, the Son of God. He will one day come through the blue. No matter where I am—it may be in the depths of the deepest ocean, on top of the highest mountain; it may be sick or well; it may be near or far; but when He comes, He is coming for me! Thank God for the millennium of His coming!

"And unto them that look for him shall he appear the second time without sin unto salvation."—Heb. 9:28.

BUILDING AND BATTLING

Two of the most difficult areas to maintain in the life of any Christian are balance and consistency. In these twelve heart-warming and stirring sermons from the pen of Dr. Curtis Hutson, you will find recipes for both.

You will immediately sense the pastor's heart in these messages first preached to his beloved congregation at Forrest Hills Baptist Church. He encourages his people to both build and battle.

The evangelistic thrust emerges as you read "Soul Winning, Every Christian's Job" and "The World's Greatest Crime."

In every message included in this book, you will notice Dr. Hutson's warm, vibrant style of preaching, his up-to-the-minute illustrations, and his heart-throbbing concern for people. You can easily see how this man of God built the great example ministry of Forrest Hills Baptist Church in Decatur, Georgia, and has now gone on to win the hearts of thousands as Editor of THE SWORD OF THE LORD and as a greatly used evangelist preaching across America.

Order two copies of BUILDING AND BATTLING, one for your own library and one to share with a friend. Any one of the twelve outstanding messages is worth more than the cost of the book.